A GROUNDBREAKING BOOK THAT OFFERS CONCRETE WAYS FOR JEWS AND PALESTINIANS TO SPEAK (AND LISTEN) DIFFERENTLY TO EACH OTHER

The Wall Between is a book about the wall that exists between Jewish and Palestinian communities in the Diaspora. Distrust, enmity, and hate are common currencies. For Jews, Israel must exist; for Palestinians, the historic injustice being committed since 1948 must be reversed. Neither wants to know why the Other cannot budge on these issues. The wall is up.

These responses emanate, primarily, from the two "metanarratives" of Jews and Palestinians: the Holocaust and the Nakba. Virtually every response to the struggle, from a member of either community, can be traced back to issues of identity, trauma, and victimhood as they relate to their respective metanarrative.

The authors utilize recent cognitive research on the psychological and social barriers that keep Jews and Palestinians in their camps, walled off from each other, and present a clear way through—one that is justice-centered, rather than trauma and propaganda-driven. The authors have lived these principles and traveled this journey, away from their tribal traumas, through embracing the principles of justice. They insist that commitment to the Other means grappling with seemingly incompatible narratives until shared values are decided and acted upon.

The Wall Between is a call to justice that challenges the status quo of Zionism while at the same time dealing directly with the complex histories that have created the situation today. It is both realistic and hopeful—a guide for anyone who is open to new possibilities within the Israel-Palestine discourse in the West.

T0112877

THE WALL BETWEEN

WHAT JEWS AND PALESTINIANS DON'T WANT TO KNOW ABOUT EACH OTHER

by Raja G. Khouri &
Jeffrey J. Wilkinson, Ph.D.

OLIVE
BRANCH
PRESS

An imprint of Interlink Publishing Group, Inc.
Northampton, Massachusetts

First published in 2023 by

Olive Branch Press
An imprint of Interlink Publishing Group, Inc.
46 Crosby Street
Northampton, Massachusetts 01060
www.interlinkbooks.com

ISBN 978-1-62371-719-3

Library of Congress Control Number: 2023941534
LC record available at https://lccn.loc.gov/2023941534

4 6 8 10 9 7 5 3

Printed and bound in the United States of America

To Thuraya Khalil

For your support and inspiration
Ann, Sara & Emilie

CONTENTS

A Note to our Readers ix

Introduction xi

Part I – Building the Wall: Shaping the Narrative

Chapter 1: How We Come to "Know" 3

Chapter 2: Memory Is More Than What Happened 9

Chapter 3: The Mortar in the Wall: Identity, Trauma, and Victimhood 13

Part II – The Bricks in the Wall: Competing Narratives

Chapter 4: Antisemitism 21

Chapter 5: Zionism and the Nakba. 43

Chapter 6: Palestinian Resistance. 67

Part III – Hardening the Wall: Weaponizing the Narrative

Chapter 7: Jewish Exceptionalism and Palestinian Otherness 91

Chapter 8: Weaponizing Tribalism 101

Part IV – Dismantling the Wall: The Making of a New Narrative

Chapter 9: Towards Values-Forward Thinking 113

Chapter 10: Working in Spaces Where the Narratives Collide. 127

Afterword. 139

Acknowledgements. 145

Endnotes 147

Bibliography and Suggested Further Reading 157

Appendix: Suggested Questions for Discussion Groups
    or Book Clubs 159

About the Authors 163

A NOTE TO OUR READERS

Throughout this book, we will frequently frame an issue or a response to an issue as "for Jews" or "for Palestinians." While we do not see these two groups as monoliths, we are speaking about the prevailing feelings and reactions among members of each tribe—their primary narratives. The reader is to assume that mentions of "Jews and "Palestinians" refer to the plurality of Jews and Palestinians, within the two Diasporas, in the general discussion about the conflict as a whole.

INTRODUCTION

"True peace is not merely the absence of tension;
it is the presence of justice."
—Dr. Martin Luther King Jr.

In 2002, during what is known as the Second Intifada, the Israeli government began work on a "separation barrier" that today covers about 700 kilometers around the 1948 cease-fire line, also known as the Green Line. If one were to do an Internet search about the wall/fence, you would be inundated with antithetical descriptions. For example, *Al Jazeera* refers to it as "an apartheid wall ... resulting in the confiscation of large swathes of Palestinian land."[1] Honest Reporting refutes that it even is a wall and calls it a "necessary fence, preventing Palestinian terrorists from killing innocent civilians."[2]

A lot can be gleaned about your position on Israel-Palestine by what you call the wall/fence and how you think about it. These positions are largely based on tribal affiliation and the media you consume, which, in turn, determine your overall disposition on the Palestinian-Israeli struggle.

While Jews and Palestinians may think often of how the wall affects them, they are much less likely to consider the Other: the one behind the wall. Within the Diasporas, we have built our own wall, keeping the Other at a distance, defending our position rather than being curious about theirs.

Tribal responses, defined by entrenched opinions and reason-proof resistance to any and all thoughts from or about the Other, have overwhelmingly dominated the Israel-Palestine discourse within the two Diasporas. (The Other is framed here as how we create or name "the other" as a group, which is why we capitalize it.) Furthermore, they have fostered an interpersonal and online chorus of grievances and victimhood statements that have come to define "them" and "us" and ensure that "our tribe" always sings from the same song sheet.

In May 2021, the fourth "Gaza War" created a shift in thinking about the Israel-Palestine struggle in some left-leaning Western circles who started recognizing the Palestinian cause as a justice issue. This book is intended as a partial antidote to the epidemic of identity-driven discourse, capitalizing on the "justice moment" we find ourselves in. While it often seems that polarization is the order of the day—which any prescribed road map to peace has come to a dead end—there is something brewing, bubbling to the surface. Opinions about the struggle are almost exclusively ideologically driven, dismissive of a contrary opinion, and backward leaning rather than forward dreaming. The endless "opinion competition" can leave us feeling hopeless and directionless, stuck in our silos, arguing rather than listening. Yet, in recent years, North America has witnessed a racial and social justice awakening, one that can be described as a justice revolution, that is not unlike the civil rights revolution of the 1960s and the human rights revolution of the 1970s. (Though we focus on North America, specifically the United States and Canada, many of the ideas we discuss are relevant to the West in general.) Encompassing Me Too, the Red Power movement in the US, the Idle No More movement in Canada, and perhaps most significantly, the Black Lives Matter (BLM) movement, these have coalesced with the Palestinian rights movement in an unprecedented way.

For many progressive Jews this is deeply disquieting, as they are generally aligned with the BLM cause and are troubled when Israel is seen in the same oppressive light as systemically racist systems here in North America.

This "justice moment" provides us all with a unique opportunity to interrupt the status quo marked by perpetual suffering and renewed traumas. In our work, we resist being ideologues but are not deterred by critiques of our idealism. We have no illusions that this path will lead to nirvana, but we are committed to offering "a way towards a way" forward that has yet to be taken. As our entrenched tribal stances were not formed overnight, there will be twists and turns in the road as we dig our way out of them. As is always the case, with new awakenings comes intensification of old resistances. We are calling for a move from *who* is right to *what* is right.

We have become not only entirely dysfunctional in our discourse; we have become undyingly loyal to this dysfunction. It is time to chart a new path, to challenge the narratives that have been so embedded that we are not really hearing each other at all.

In July 2020, Peter Beinart, a journalism professor and prominent liberal Zionist, published an article in *Jewish Currents* entitled "Yavne: A Jewish Case for Equality in Israel-Palestine." The article caused quite a stir, particularly in liberal Jewish circles, as Beinart explicitly called on Jews to accept that the two-state solution was no longer feasible, and the only path forward was a single state, with equal rights for its Jewish and Palestinian citizens.

Beinart's call, which resonates much more loudly after the events of spring 2021,[3] can be restated as a call to see the real-life consequences of the status quo, especially for Palestinians living "behind the wall," without basic freedoms or hope for justice and a fair outcome in the foreseeable future. Seeing behind the wall is not an esoteric exercise, but an urgent need. There are dire consequences, for both peoples, in remaining invisible to each other.

This book looks deeply at the reasons why we have remained in our camps, resistant to the Other's realities while also calling on all of us to not only see the Other but to become invested in achieving a just outcome for all.

At present, neither a one-democratic-state nor a two-separate-states solution seems feasible. The reality is that, for many Jews, the two-state solution remains a comforting idea to hang on to, although its realization has become virtually unattainable. This book both acknowledges this and charts a path towards calling for justice for all the people of the land.

We are attempting to open a gateway to the Other, what many may see as a form of "bridge-building." While this term typically denotes a sense of building empathy for the Other by giving equal consideration to each narrative in question, our aim is to shed light on the places where we are unable to fully see or truly understand the Other.

Our framework is premised on the understanding that most Jews have had far less exposure to the Palestinian narrative than Palestinians have had to the Jewish narrative—although this is beginning to shift. Furthermore, the vast majority of Americans and Canadians have had far greater exposure to, and understanding of, the Jewish narrative than the Palestinian one. While there are many reasons for this, the most straightforward explanation is that the Jewish narrative has been told at a far greater frequency and effectiveness than the Palestinian one, thanks to the plethora of representations in literature, films, plays, TV, and other media, along with well-executed institutionalized efforts. As a result, the Jewish narrative has become part of the mainstream culture and discourse in North America, whereas the Palestinian narrative has not. We explore the reasons for this later in the book. The less we know about the Other, the less we are able to understand them.

The "wall" between the two sides must be dismantled before a "bridge" to the Other can be constructed. For this dismantling to occur, all those engaged must enter into the uncomfortable process of seeing beyond their preconceptions. It requires resisting simple tropes about the Other that are promulgated through misleading and often-disparaging information disseminated by forces determined to maintain the wall within.

Bridging the divide between the two communities is an act of optimism and hope, driven by a commitment to our shared Western values of respect, inclusion, and dignity for all. This work must not be left to Jews and Palestinians exclusively. The cycle of blame and retribution has left a scar on the human spirit. While this book focuses on Israel-Palestine and the debate within the respective Diasporas, the cycle of blame is emblematic of a larger schism in Western society where we align with one at the expense of another. We reject this paradigm. Social justice movements are replete with examples of systems of oppression resisting on one level and cooperating on another. The rights and dignity of an oppressed group must become enmeshed with our own rights and dignity. Our freedom and the freedom of another are intrinsically linked.

We detail both Palestinian and Jewish narratives in order to frame empathetic listening and bridge-building as a path toward justice and reconciliation, rather than pabulum for those who want simple answers to complex questions. In other words, much has been said about fostering coexistence, but what is needed is "co-resistance." The source of this phrase is Jonathan Kuttab, a Palestinian leader in peacemaking who used this term to delineate events that foster togetherness between Jews and Palestinians in Israel-Palestine, asking Jews to become active in standing against the unjust treatment of Palestinians. We are applying this to dialogue work "over here." Dialogue groups within the Diasporas have long sought to understand each other, but this has not moved the needle in any useful way. In this book, we see understanding as an important first step, but it can't be the end game.

This book began from a conversation between the authors that led to another conversation and another and another. This was never a conversation about the Other, but rather a conversation with the Other. We practiced and continue to practice listening, questioning, learning, and growing. It is not that we never disagree or struggle, but rather that our commitment to working together is greater than our need to be right. We talk to each other with the nagging awareness that we just don't know what we think we know.

Indifference breeds in spaces where others live outside of your reality. One becomes the Other only by our actions or inactions. Our work in this book is about how the wall has formed, how this distance continues to widen, and how we might, first, peer over, and then dismantle the metaphorical wall within us. When we meet and begin to know the Other, we create the possibility for "them" to become part of our "we."

Many actions that were taken during the Trump administration—the "Deal of the Century" (the Abraham Accords), moving the American embassy to Jerusalem, new threats of annexing large parts of the West Bank—have taken "othering" to the place where one doesn't even consider the needs or views of the Other, or even recognize that the Other exists. As we describe in detail in this book, it is indicative of the tribal bubble that has become the norm in this discourse.

We are meeting you where you are. You may be Jewish or Palestinian or an interested party invested in this discourse. By choosing to read this book, you must, at least in some way, be frustrated and/or disenchanted with the state of the current discourse and want to begin a different conversation, beyond your tribal belonging and the narrative that came with it. You may still feel trapped in your bubble, or you may have burst out of it; you're at the very least, questioning it. Many of us have been in this conversation for many years. Some have shifted their way of thinking entirely, and some are earlier in the journey of listening beyond the noise, peering over the wall. Our gateway to the Other is laid out in such a way that you can join the journey wherever you are. If you are reading this book, we expect that you are already on this journey and are curious about where it can take you.

A key tension throughout this book is how to resist the injustices in Palestine-Israel today, especially in Gaza and the West Bank, and still ask Palestinians to engage with Jews and Jewish trauma. This is not an either-or proposition; we must both speak out against injustice and engage in deepening our understanding of the Other.

For some, this may appear to be a form of equivocation: "Both sides suffer, and both have a reasonable story." However, in the discourse in North America, the power balance is so heavily weighted to the pro-Israel position that alleviating the suffering of Palestinians is often left out of the conversation. Because most of the body politic in both the US and Canada is deeply sympathetic to historic Jewish suffering, the Holocaust experience, and ongoing antisemitism, sympathy regularly translates to near-unequivocal support for Israel.

If these statements challenge you, it may be a sign that your position usually goes unquestioned.

Yes, we want Palestinians to engage with Jews and to resist simplistic and demonizing statements like "Jews are an evil menace and the sole cause of our suffering," which are common in some anti-Israel propaganda. This is counterproductive to creating a space where mutual understanding and a shared vision can develop. Jews and Palestinians have come to share a destiny, one with colliding visions and broken dreams. Only a shared vision can usher in a different future.

Jews and Palestinians, since the late nineteenth century, would view each other as the Other, but this otherness is not predetermined; it results from narrow identifications that encourage who we are not, rather than who we are. This book is written by a Palestinian and a Jew, but it is about two narratives rather than two identities. Narratives marked by belonging and un-belonging, by wounds and joys, by setbacks and accomplishments.

We are aware that many of our readers will have nuanced views about the struggle. Many Jews may be critical of Israeli policies but still identify as Zionists. Many Palestinians may be critical of the Palestinian leadership yet are still deeply committed to Palestinian liberation. As you read, avoid separating yourself from a particular statement, as nothing we say here applies universally to every Jew or every Palestinian.

This book is not intended to be a complete review of the long and winding history of the Israeli/Palestinian struggle, nor of Jews and Palestinians themselves. We lay out a general historical context only to show how we have come to our often-polarized stances. In the end, though, this is not primarily a look back, rather a look forward.

We are working on two levels: First, to bring a deeper understanding to Jews and Palestinians, specifically within their respective Diasporas, of how and why the Other responds to events the way they do. But this is just the first step. We also need to shift the discourse in the larger body politic and citizenry, particularly in the United States Canada, and Europe, tilting the scales towards justice. Our aspiration is to engage all those with a concern for peace, social justice, and human rights in looking deeply at the Israel-Palestine discourse in North America and becoming engaged with it through this lens.

The first step in understanding the intractable nature in which Jews and Palestinians respond to each other is to examine their two respective metanarratives—the overarching stories that inform all other stories of an individual or a group—the Holocaust and the Nakba.

In *The Holocaust and the Nakba: A New Grammar of Trauma and History*, editors Bashir and Goldberg bring together writings that explore these two narratives, both their similarities and their differences.[4] What is most significant for the reader is not the "correctness" of each narrative, but how the narrative informs the Other and the Other's position. Like Bashir and Goldberg, we view historical trauma and the resulting sense of victimhood, for both Jews and Palestinians, as byproducts of these two metanarratives.

The voluminous output on this subject, in books, articles, blogs, tweets, posts, etc., seems to fall into three general categories. The first are works that are unabashedly pro-Israel and wholly supportive of Zionism. They present historical justifications for where we are today and argue that Zionism is the only remedy for past and current antisemitism. These writings paint Palestinians as irrevocably malevolent and terroristic and the Palestinian leadership unsuitable as a partner for peace. Israel is seen as the victim of an Arab behemoth that is bent on destroying the Jewish state. These writings are fodder for the pro-Israel lobby, deepening the divide between us, rather than attempting to bring us together.

In another group are works that are clearly pro-Palestinian, most commonly written by left-leaning academics and often focusing on settler-colonialism, apartheid, and the Occupation. Also, these writings often frame the debate in terms of race: white settlers imposing their will on people of color. These writings give an extremely valuable historical perspective, particularly for Jews (and others) who have not been exposed to this counternarrative. While our views generally align with the social justice frameworks of these writings, we are focused primarily on understanding the Other through a justice lens, rather than what can be viewed as disparaging or demonizing.

A third group are works that come from a primarily Jewish/Israeli perspective and can be framed as "pro-Israel and pro-peace," usually written by self-described "progressive Zionists." Driven by a sense of social justice and human rights, these writers intentionally resist all-or-nothing approaches to the discussion. Their stance is somewhat nuanced, stating a clear commitment to a just future for Palestinians and Jews. However, these writings often focus on the need to share the Jewish narrative with Palestinians. They tend to justify the Jewish/Israeli narrative as a way of explaining the need for a Jewish state, while still supporting Palestinian rights. This form of bridge-building, in our view, is destined to bear little fruit, as it ignores the deep discrepancies in power and influence between Israelis and Palestinians and, ultimately, puts Israel's existence as a Jewish-majority state ahead of any meaningful redress and historic justice for Palestinians.

An example of this is *Letters to My Palestinian Neighbor*, by Yossi Klein Halevi, which reaches across the ethnic and political divide in an effort to close the gap between "them" and "us." He is clearly sincere in his intentions to show empathy for Palestinians, yet he also wants to inform them of Jewish history and what many Israeli Jews fear from the Palestinian resistance movement.

We highlight Halevi's book to draw a clear distinction between what he and many other Jewish progressives have attempted and what we are doing here. Halevi is looking for a partner in peace and clearly suggests that the Palestinian leadership has not seriously engaged in this. Many Jewish progressives have seized on his book to ask why there are no "letters" from Palestinians. Our focus is on developing a shared dialogue within a social justice framework that recognizes the need for Palestinians to understand Jewish historical trauma but doesn't mitigate the injustices done to them; rather, one that opens spaces where one might view the Other differently.

A key contributor to our indifference to the Other is our need to have our experiences and "truths" acknowledged. There is competition between hearing another's story and quieting, or even silencing, our own.

While it is understandable for Halevi to want to "teach" Palestinians about Jewish history, and specifically Jewish trauma, this can be read as a form of silencing the pleas of Palestinians for their own suffering to be heard. This, of course, happens conversely, when Jews react to Palestinians who talk of 1948 solely from the perspective of what they lost, without recognizing that the Jewish state was created as a haven for Jews after centuries of suffering, culminating with the Holocaust.

In other words, the need to have our stories heard often prevents us from hearing the stories of the Other. Our resistance to the Other results, in part, from muting the Other's story and amplifying our own. We create space for our own narrative by limiting space for the Other's narrative.

We trust that Jews and Palestinians (and others) who read our book will learn much about the other, but our goal is not to justify, but rather to illuminate. When a Jew tells a Palestinian what they need, it is a difficult pill to swallow for a group that has lost so much. We are not asking Palestinians and Jews to enter into peace talks; we are encouraging everyone to listen first, keep an open mind, peer over the wall, think outside their bubble, and engage with difficult learning. Peace, sadly, can't really be considered until we understand and address the inequity gaps that exist today between Israelis and Palestinians, and the extent to which justice has been denied to Palestinians in the past century. Halevi's (and many other progressive voices) need to protect Israel as a Jewish majority state consistently overwhelms their calls for peace and understanding, thereby preventing the kind of deep learning that is needed to alter the situation on the ground.

This book leans heavily on a conversation geared towards replacing our tribal lenses with lenses of justice and the freedom values we cherish. With the power differential in the current discourse being so immense, we resist the "both-sideism" that is commonplace in progressive-leaning Jewish discourse. Most importantly, learning and understanding the Other does not mean equivocation. Shared experience does not mean shared impact. We ask the reader to wrestle with multiple truths: Antisemitism has been and continues to be a blight on the Jewish experience, and living with dispossession and under oppression is a weight on Palestinians that just can't be equated with today's antisemitism.

While there are many ways to define the reasons for the intractable struggle in Israel-Palestine/Palestine-Israel, we focus on the "struggle about the struggle," specifically in North America. On any given day, one can read dozens of opinion pieces where North American pundits weigh in on the "conflict," usually presented within the context of the tribe the author identifies with. (We generally stay away from using the word "conflict" as this term, for many, implies equivalency between combatants, rather than a struggle between an oppressed and an oppressor. We will usually use the word "struggle" instead.) In fact, the Israel-Palestine debate has fostered its own media machine, cranking out diatribes, often laden with misinformation, hyperbole, and emotional alarmism. Some promote solutions, but most exacerbate the tribal divide, using human and financial capital to prove the veracity of their side and diminish the Other. (Imagine what would be possible if the power of the Diaspora would instead be used to create and promote a vision for a shared future?)

We offer that the universal antagonism between Jews and Palestinians appears to the North American eye as one between what we call "mainstreamed muscularity" and "marginalized resistance." This is a dichotomous relationship that pushes and pulls against the Other, creating a cycle of intransigence that becomes a self-fulfilling prophecy that ensures inaction.

Too often, fault seems to be the focus of our discussions, defined mostly along tribal lines. What we will lay out here is the image of mainstreamed muscularity that defines the Jewish pro-Israel lobby exerts its power in a manner that dismisses Palestinians and the Palestinian cause, all the while appearing more rational, more democratic and more just. Furthermore, Palestinian frustration and disillusionment are often displayed as anger, radicalism, and rejectionism—marginalized resistance, which plays into and supports the mainstream nature of the pro-Israel lobby.

It is important to recognize too that there is a Palestinian youth movement that is highly organized and effective. Also, while the movement for Boycott, Divestment, and Sanctions (BDS), which we'll discuss in Chapter 4, has not yet had a deep impact on the Israeli economy or academia, it too is organized and deliberate. It is essential to understand that the power and scope of the pro-Israel lobby presents itself as righteously muscular, having some predestined moral authority, in contrast to segments of the Palestinian resistance that lack the political clout to change the trajectory of mainstream discourse.

While the Jewish and Palestinian narratives are juxtaposed in terms of power, one muscular and one marginalized, their roots are decidedly similar. We identify three specific psychosocial energies, or "mortar in the wall," that are shared by Palestinians and Jews but work to further separate us rather than bring us together. These are "identity" (who we are and who we are not), "trauma" (repeated wounding that continues to reverberate in the present), and "victimhood" (the result of long-term trauma that has us view the world from a victim perspective). These separate phenomena also intertwine with and magnify the impact they have on each tribe.

It is essential to separate the historical experiences of trauma and victimhood from an evaluation of the current impact on each group. Stated differently, understanding the traumatic past of the Other is never a justification for current inequalities. Rather, it is a vehicle towards being able to peer above the wall and develop a more just foundation for the way we relate to the Other.

Sadly, much of the discourse today is driven by ideologically centered groups who use their significant clout to stoke tribally driven narratives, evoking deep feelings of victimhood that prevent their readers and listeners from healing. These groups use tropes and misinformation to politicize and weaponize victimhood. This not only greatly deepens the divide between us, it also entrenches the notion of being under constant attack from the Other and inflames trauma for the purpose of pushing a particular agenda.

While both sides employ these strategies, we will show how the pro-Israel lobby works from a well-funded, highly organized and muscular position that exacerbates the narrative of a fragmented and, in some cases, poorly led Palestinian resistance.

THE PATHWAY

The book is divided into four parts, showing how the narrative was shaped (the mortar in the wall), the competing narratives that exist (the bricks in the wall), the weaponization of the narrative (the barbed wire around the wall), and the new narrative needed (for dismantling the wall).

Part I – "Building the Wall: Shaping the Narrative" examines how we have come to our positions and how the isolation between us has occurred. We look here at how we come to know, and how this "knowing" becomes tribalized and grows resistant to new learning, giving particular attention to the three elements we referred to earlier that make up the mortar in the wall: identity, trauma, and victimhood.

Part II – "The Bricks in the Wall: Competing Narratives" deals primarily with three big ideas: antisemitism, Zionism and the Nakba, and Palestinian resistance, and how most Jews and Palestinians view these concepts entirely differently. In each case, what is seen as a fight against tyranny by one group is seen as a repetition of historical oppression by the other. Antisemitism, while understandably viewed by Jews as a system of beliefs and actions that target them, is seen by Palestinians as a weapon being used to silence their resistance to oppression. Zionism is both the realization of a Jewish homeland and the force destroying the dream of a Palestinian homeland. Palestinian resistance is a movement of national solidarity for one group and the threat of annihilation for the other.

In Part III – "Hardening the Wall: Weaponizing the Narrative" articulates how media representations employ propaganda, foment identity politics, and weaponize trauma and victimhood by singing from the Jewish or Palestinian songbooks, evoking the worst aspects of tribal thinking in both groups.

Part IV – "Dismantling the Wall: The Making of a New Narrative" charts a beginning course out of the static status quo by suggesting a narrative that is free from the influence of identity, trauma and victimhood, resistant to propaganda wars and groupthink, one that is based on the values we hold dear as citizens of liberal democracies: freedom, respect, dignity, equality, and human rights. We offer a transformative approach, driven by an idealistic vision but supported by pragmatic pathways out of the traps that have created the downward spiral, away from the Other, and away from justice.

This writing holds multiple truths: Both Jews and Palestinians have a traumatic past and have endured great pain and victimization that must be understood better by the Other. Yet, understanding alone will not create a better and more peaceful future. We know that conflict is, in part, a natural relational "us vs. them" phenomenon that is rooted in how we process knowledge, filter information, and remember our individual and collective histories.

Throughout the book, the reader is asked to push the boundaries of tribal expectation, to risk knowing disquieting truths, and to include the narrative of the Other within their own. Individually and tribally, we tend to see our stories in a way that excludes the Other's stories, leaving us on separate paths, only concerned for ourselves.

Many Palestinians and academics on the left are driven by a view of Zionism as a strictly settler-colonial enterprise. Most Jews and mainstream North America, on the other hand, are driven by the conviction that Zionism is a Jewish nationalist project. We, in this book, choose to be driven by justice, rather than tribal ideology. A just view recognizes that, after centuries of European oppression and victimization, the desire for security drove a nationalist Jewish project of self-determination on what many Jews considered their ancestral homeland. Yet, by accepting that this project would displace and dispossess the existing Palestinian population, Zionism in effect behaved, and in its outcome was identical to, any other colonial endeavor.

WHO SHOULD READ THIS BOOK?

This book is aimed at people who come from many different perspectives on the Israel-Palestine struggle here in North America. It is for you who care about this issue, no matter where you currently are on the subject, and are willing to challenge what you know, or think you know, about Jews and Palestinians, and the struggle as a whole. In our work we have articulated a particular need, even in the progressive-leaning community, to push past common misconceptions about the Other and to move towards a cooperative model of co-ownership and co-action. This book is for people in the Jewish and Palestinian Diasporas, but also for the many others who have become engaged in the dilemma that is Israel-Palestine. You may be seeking ways to understand and experience another's trauma and find ways to use this to work together. You may have already forged a common purpose with another that reaches beyond your personal and tribal experiences of trauma. Or you may simply be tired of the status quo, the decades of enmity and suffering, the hate and vitriol, and in search of an alternative path that is unhindered by stale, tired, and ultimately disastrous conventional wisdom.

No matter where you see yourself, this is a book for the curious and reflective, for those seeking to expand their knowledge, those who are driven by values of decency and are fed up with the indecency of the status quo—for those committed to justice as a pathway for peace.

If you consider yourself "progressive," you may think that you already see and listen to the Other "behind the wall." Yet we are all resistant to the Other in some areas, particularly in places where trauma and the threat of the recurrence of trauma are triggered.

THE DILEMMA

First, we need to state clearly that this book is for the Jewish and Palestinian Diaspora communities and those participating in the Israel-Palestine discourse, as a whole, in North America and elsewhere. It is not aimed at those living in Palestine-Israel. The prime importance of this is so that we focus on our interactions in the United States, Canada, and other parts of the Diasporas, where there is a certain distance from the daily strains of the Occupation and the struggle over there.

That said, trauma does transcend distance and time. Palestinians in the Diaspora are themselves descendants of 1948 refugees, or have lived under the Occupation, or have families living under it. Also, there are Diaspora Jews who, separate from the tremendous losses in the Holocaust, have had intimate experiences with a loved one dying as a soldier in the Israeli army or from a violent attack.

Indifference to the Other and the Other's needs exists in both camps; there is no debating this. The consequences of this indifference to the Other in the two communities can be examined without equating the conditions on the ground between Israelis and Palestinians. In other words, the scope of the suffering of Palestinians, caused in part by the resistance of Jews and much of Western society to engage with it, doesn't preclude us from being empathetic to Israelis who have also suffered physical and emotional loss.

We are working with a conundrum. We each want the Other to hear us differently, but many are unaware of where the Other is coming from. Each wants something from the Other but is waiting for the Other to move first. Palestinian rights and Jewish rights have become dependent on each other, and one cannot be achieved without the other.

We call for a discourse that resists identity-driven, ideologically based thinking, motivated instead by our desire for justice and support for human rights. The authors understand that the reader, like most of us, has learned to view this struggle from a relatively narrow perspective and will likely be challenged by our process, a challenge we encourage you to wholly embrace.

We reject the status quo in its entirety. Instead, we embrace the possibility of a new discourse, based on the common values we hold dear and devoid of the rhetoric and browbeating we have regularly been engaged in. We see all of us as wounded, separate from the cause of the wounding.

In order to engage fully with the text, please keep these five questions in the back of your mind as you read:

1. Is my cultural/ethnic/religious identity informing my stance?
2. Is there a trauma (wound) that is being re-experienced?
3. Am I viewing this through a victim lens?
4. If I am not Jewish or Palestinian, are Western guilt and/or resistance to the Other's narrative at play when I hear new information?
5. Is the stance I'm holding true to the values I proclaim to hold dear?

Remember, as you do this, whether as a Jew or a Palestinian or another interested party, none of us is immune to the forces of identity, trauma, and victimhood. Tribalism is communal and is a manifestation of our belonging to something, but it is also being used as a powerful force for division, resistance to the Other and the Other's trauma, and for the defense of ongoing injustice. Information can expand or narrow our thinking. We get to choose which one it is. Embrace the challenge!

—Raja and Jeff

PART I – BUILDING THE WALL: SHAPING THE NARRATIVE

"He drew a circle that shut me out – Heretic, rebel, a thing to flout.
But love and I had the wit to win: We drew a circle and took him in!"
—Edwin Markham, from the poem "Outwitted"

CHAPTER 1
HOW WE COME TO "KNOW"

"Everyone you will ever meet knows something that you don't."
—Bill Nye

It is undeniable that "the struggle about the struggle" in Israel-Palestine has walled us off in our camps. We have our opinions, they have their opinions. More starkly, we have the truth and they have their ill-informed beliefs. Abject disagreement and rejection of differing viewpoints are commonplace. We "know" what we "know," and have amassed "evidence" to convince another of the veracity of what we "know."

The struggle between the two Diasporas (and between their supporters), like the separation wall did not occur all at once. Constructing the metaphorical wall between us is not an event, but a process, one that has occurred slowly over decades, passed on from one generation to the next, so that we have not likely noticed its scope or consequence.

As we will show, the wall is not just between Jews and Palestinians and those deeply engaged in the Israel-Palestine conversation, but within the broader societal and political structures in the West. Our general view of Arabs (and Muslims in general) has tilted our perception of the struggle over there. We have taken sides even though

3

we may not be fully aware of it. We know who is part of "us" and who belongs to "them."

There are many truisms that demonstrate how our divisions block us from hearing and seeing the Other. These have overwhelmed the conversation in the struggle about the struggle within the two Diasporas, such as, "Jews control the North American media so it's always on their side." "There is no end to Israel's nefariousness." "The Arab world is massive—why can't they let Jews have their little piece of land?" "It was the Arabs who attacked Israel in 1948."

These statements are very familiar. Each of them (and dozens more) frames "us" as opposed to "them." They did it, and are doing it, not us.

We know we are right or mostly right, and we are not going to be swayed by the Other's propaganda. Meanwhile, we seem unconcerned about the propaganda coming from our own camp.

Being inured to the plight of another is unpleasant for us to own up to. But we have, in large part, become resistant to information we find uncomfortable, or that runs counter to our positions. We have become immune to the Other and the Other's narrative.

What is less known is how this has occurred. Why do we seek information that confirms our positions, when it is through exposure to new ideas that growth occurs? Why are we so sure of ourselves and our "facts?" Why do we so naturally assume that another's narrative is somehow less important than our own? Why do we often attribute malice to the Other's motives but not to our own?

What has happened? How did this entrenchment in our own ways of thinking come to repel us from unsettling ideas? What are the factors that keep us apart?

It is not that we are stubborn, recalcitrant, and unable to learn, but that a wall has formed between us, created by the psychological and social tensions at work in each of us and in our tribes. It begins with how we seek information and how we process it.

A common tension in debates with others we disagree with is that, while we may have a surface awareness that we are wired to elevate our story and debase another's, we really do believe that "truth" is on our side. Even in dialogue with another, our tendency is to listen in order to respond rather than listen to understand. We may be calling something a dialogue when it is more like two simultaneous monologues.

While we live in a knowledge-based world, we are selective about what knowledge we seek. We have millions of facts and figures available to us through a simple Google search, so how do we select what we learn about? Is this a random process? Highly unlikely. If we were to each track our social media history, a pattern would likely emerge, showing our general interests, our likes and dislikes, and our political, religious, and cultural affiliations.

While resistance to knowledge that runs counter to our positions and beliefs is quite natural, we need to better understand where this comes from. Cognitive science teaches us that humans, from the beginning of time, have naturally resisted the new and unfamiliar. The stranger and the strange thing are often processed in the brain as danger. Likewise, the Other, or those who are not only outside of our circle but whose narrative is in conflict with ours, are seen through the "danger" lens. Most of us feel that we have evolved to the point where we welcome new learning and are committed to personal and societal growth. There is, however, this natural resistance in us to uncomfortable information, and some information creates more resistance than other information.

If we are to seize this "moment of justice," created by a fresh awareness of injustice and inequalities, we need to address how we come to know, and, most importantly, how to "know" differently.

CONFIRMATION BIAS AND BELIEF PERSEVERANCE

We learn from social psychologists that certain opportunities for new learning, often in our subconscious thinking, are subjected to extra screening. They are being put through what might best be described as a "conformity test." We know about confirmation bias (seeking information that agrees with our preconceived notions), but somehow we seem to be naturally more aware of it in others rather than in ourselves.

This process of confirmation, over time, begins at a subconscious level. The brain is a pattern maker, learning by making a series of connections. This pattern making helps us learn new things by building on what we already know. However, when we encounter information that fits a previously held belief, the brain's pattern-making ability can shield us from critically evaluating a new idea. For example, if you are sent a news item showing a Palestinian protesting in Jerusalem and you are predisposed to think that all Palestinians are terroristic, you are then less likely to question the meaning or legitimacy of what the Palestinian is protesting. Similarly, if you believe Israel is a settler-colonial military state, when you are sent a post claiming an Israeli soldier has done something terrible to a Palestinian child, you are inclined to believe it at face value, not necessarily concerning yourself with the source of the information and/or its validity. When we encounter new information, if it resonates within our predisposition on the subject, it is processed and stored in our "ideological memory," without much or any critical thinking.

It is a natural human instinct, if unchecked, to overvalue our own experiences, ideas, and beliefs over those of another, and to filter new information through a confirmation bias lens. So, what do we do with the idea of widening our circle, as Edwin Markham's short poem at the start of this section suggests?

As an illustration, consider that you have likely seen posts on Facebook or other media that you wholly disagreed with or that challenged your "truth." For example, what would you think of a post that described climate change as a leftist conspiracy meant to dampen the free-market economy? For some, this would be seen as conservative drivel, making them feel puzzled, perhaps angered, and resistant. For others, this may be confirmation of their own view and they find it comforting. Regardless of your position, your confirmation bias either enshrines your view that all climate change deniers are kooks, or that all liberals are crazy. Your circle narrows.

While confirmation bias is the tendency to look for, interpret, and remember information according to your beliefs, belief perseverance is the phenomenon of sticking with a belief, even if the belief is proven to be fallacious. Stereotypical views of Jews and Palestinians/Arabs seem, like a particularly virulent strain of a communicable virus, deeply resistant to the antibiotic of new learning. If we have held notions of the Other, entrenched over time, particularly when they are politically advantageous to our tribe, we are likely not to be swayed by new evidence. This phenomenon—resisting new learning, coupled with confirmation bias—of seeking information that gels with our preconceived ideas, builds a wall between us and then layers it with a hardened lacquer, making it close to impenetrable. Markham, instead, suggests that the width of the circle is not determined by what you are confronted with, but rather what you choose to do with it. What we include in our circle, which may encompass beliefs and ideas we are repelled by if we choose to, is within our control. In other words, agreeing and including are different. You could engage in respectful curiosity, seeking to understand rather than to disagree. Being exposed to new knowledge is not, in itself, dangerous. Rather, it is an opportunity to widen our circle of understanding.

There is a potential danger in discussing the inherent nature of confirmation bias and belief perseverance: that we will use this as an excuse to remain in our camps. While we have become accustomed to viewing knowledge from a narrow, protective place, this is not predestined. We call on you to push past the comfortable, as seeking justice for the Other will require us to not only rethink our positions, but actually to give something up.

THE CULTURE OF "SAFETYISM"

In *The Coddling of the American Mind*, Greg Lukianoff and Jonathan Haidt tackle the growing trend of seeing uncomfortable knowledge on college and university campuses as dangerous—what they refer to as a culture of "safetyism." The authors are describing a current trend in society where physical and emotional safety have become conflated, where disquieting knowledge is believed to be dangerous, like an unsafe building or a threatening intruder.[5]

In Jewish/Palestinian discussions, particularly around the struggle, this sense of danger is fueled by the traumatic histories of the two groups, where knowledge that may lead to new ways of thinking, and even new actions, may feel dangerous. Seeing the Other and the Other's story as dangerous is not about the danger of physical harm, but rather the emotional danger it elicits—a fear that knowing the Other's plight might cause us to face things we would rather not acknowledge.

If new learning is dangerous, then how are we ever to grow and expand our circle? Our knowledge is limited by our exposure and our exposure is limited, often, by our fear. What we know is in our memory; the stories and experiences that we can recall and retell. The culture of "safetyism" Lukianoff and Haidt outline can be vividly observed in how Jews and Palestinians "identify with" the stories of their own tribes and resist those of the Other.

We come to know through exposure, repetition, and our natural bias towards information that reaffirms our place and position in the world. Our gaps in understanding become harder to detect. We build our personal and tribal stories based on what we have heard throughout our lives. What we remember and how we remember can be called our "collective memory." This plays a very important role in guiding what information we seek and how we filter that information.

In the next chapter, we will reflect on the process of remembering and how this has contributed to constructing the wall between.

CHAPTER 2
MEMORY IS MORE THAN WHAT HAPPENED

"There is no word in Hebrew for history.
The closest is zechira—*remembrance."* [6]

We can think of memory as the encyclopedia of information that we recall in telling our stories. Memory, like knowledge, is not neutral. Memory is a part of what has happened, but not all of it. Memory could perhaps be better called what is left after forgetting.

As Israel-Palestine gets so much attention, it is especially important to understand that the vast amount of material available is not "pure history," but rather selected portions of what is possible to know. Those who dedicate a great deal of time to the history of the Israeli-Palestinian struggle rely on facts and, in general, are resistant to seeing truth as malleable. [7] Of course, there are immutable solid truths, but in the context of listening to, learning from, and understanding the Other, it is essential to know that what we have come to believe is based on many factors—not only what we know as truths. Historical evidence is part of what we base our opinions on, but our principles, beliefs, and social belonging also play an important role.

As an example, consider books on the 1948 war that promote differing facts about the same event. In an academic library, one might find many books on the Deir Yassin massacre. [8] In one

9

Canadian university library, one can find a book entitled *The Birth of a Palestinian Nation: The Myth of the Deir Yassin Massacre* (Milstein, 2012), and another, *Remembering Deir Yassin: The Future of Israel and Palestine* (Ellis & McGowan, 1998), right beside it. Theoretically, these accounts are both based on factual recollections of the event at Deir Yassin during the 1948 war, but the details that are selected vary as greatly as the conclusions that they come to. Milstein is looking back and resisting what he sees as a false rationale for Palestine, while Ellis and McGowan view the past as a lesson that can help construct a different future.

Our predisposition to one side or the other will likely determine which book we are drawn to. Similar to the Facebook post on climate change, our confirmation bias, or our belief perseverance, is at play. We either chose the book we did because the title aligned with our bias on the subject, or we started both books and then put down the one that challenged our preconceptions.

However, in this case, we aren't just reinforcing and defending our ideas as individuals, but as participants in a group. Belonging to a group helps us feel centered. They are not just our stories, but also our tribe's stories. They help us carve out a space in the world within which we feel comfortable and where we belong.

Naturally, there are contested facts in most accounts of historical events, including Deir Yassin. It isn't hard to grasp that one is more likely to seek stories and retain facts that fit with what they have been taught and that also connect them to their group. What we need to wrestle with is why some stories seem more real and ring true, whereas other stories are seen as less believable or false. We privilege these stories, ascribing to them a greater level of importance within our tribe's narrative. They resonate with us. This functions much like our passion for our favorite sports team. When recalling a game that went our way, we rejoice and feel we deserved to win; conversely, when remembering a defeat at the hands of our greatest rival, we feel cheated and indulge ourselves in the memories of the loss.

Our social media intake, like the books on Deir Yassin, is selected and ingested based largely on where we come from on the issue of

Israel-Palestine. In trying to understand the polarization that exists today in politics, it is often said, "Where you stand is based on where you sit." Similarly, where you stand on Palestine-Israel determines what you read, and what and whom you listen to.

As individuals, we all have our stories, and together they become our tribe's stories. This repository of stories, our collective memory, is a way for our group to understand the past, and it plays an important role in how we have come to see ourselves and how we see those outside of our own group.

Perhaps the most important distinction between history and memory is that history is, by definition, in the past, yet memory is contemporary—it is happening. When we say, "I remember …," we are lulled into a sense that we are recalling a concrete past rather than retelling that past event in the present.

This book presents two distinctly different narratives about the past. These narratives are retellings of the past, susceptible to bias and interpretation, rather than a reliable accounting of historical facts.

Our argument is that our views on antisemitism,[9] Zionism and the Nakba, or Palestinian resistance are skewed by our natural need to seek out the familiar and resist the unfamiliar. Our collective stories act as a force field, keeping us safe and secure in what we already know, and create the "wall" between our tribes. These stories are memories, not history. This awareness alone is the essential first step in challenging our narratives.

One description of how this disconnect forms is that we are each entrenched in our personal and group identities and have both suffered long-term traumas. These traumas, which have fostered a pattern of personal and tribal victimhood, work to widen the distance between "us" and "them." In Chapter 3, we look at three distinct psychosocial phenomena that we refer to as "the mortar" in the wall, each intensifying the other, adding to the thickness, width, and impenetrability of the wall: identity, trauma, and victimhood. These influence what we remember and how we remember. They play a key role in our decision to seek some knowledge and to filter out other knowledge.

CHAPTER 3
THE MORTAR IN THE WALL:
IDENTITY, TRAUMA, AND VICTIMHOOD

IDENTITY

"All of the massacres that have taken place in recent years, like most of the bloody wars, have been linked to complex and long-standing 'cases' of identity ... for people directly involved in conflicts arising out of identity, for those who have suffered and been afraid, nothing else exists except 'them' and 'us,' the insult and the atonement."
—Amin Maalouf, *In the Name of Identity: Violence and the Need to Belong* (1998)

"Who we are" can be called our identity. This identity forms over time through a combination of familial and cultural exposures and experiences. It is more than our individual identity, as it expands beyond our personal experiences to include our cultural, ethnic, or religious tribe; it is our "social identity," or how we see ourselves in the world. This, in addition to who we are and are not, defines who we "belong" to and who we do not. Our social identity is part of what drives us to ward off unfamiliar stories and opinions while continuing to seek out stories and opinions that align with what we have learned as part of the group.

The stories that have particular significance for us and our group can be seen as "privileged memories," in that they hold a special place in our hearts and minds. While being Jewish or Palestinian is not the entirety of one's identity, in terms of the struggle and how we talk about the struggle, they are the identities that are most at play.

These identities are not preferences, as in our preference for rocky road over pralines and cream ice cream, or our cheering for the New York Yankees over the Boston Red Sox, but rather how, and to what, we belong. These identities are tied to our "sacred values," the core of us that is nonnegotiable and threats to it are existential in nature.

Being Jewish is not a preference but a belonging—a sacred value. A natural tribal connection to Israel is thereby not a preferred "flavor" for Jews, but central to what it means to be Jewish and to belong to the Jewish tribe. Stories of Palestinian hardship may be met with skepticism, as an acceptance of that hardship may threaten what many Jews feel they need in order to be safe and complete.

To a Palestinian, their identity is not a choice, but rather a controversial political statement. Being Palestinian comes with layers of complexity involving loyalty and commitment to their historic struggle: the Nakba, resistance to occupation, the memory of loss, and the omnipresent violence in their lives that necessitates their resistance. Similar to how Jews resist the stories of Palestinian oppression, Palestinians are resistant to the Jewish history of oppression since they see it as the rationale, used again and again, to oppress and dispossess them. Resistance is then a sacred value to Palestinians.

TRAUMA

"Because he was a Jew, my father died in Auschwitz" —Sara Kofman

The next layer that works to keep us apart is our past and present wounds, or trauma. For our purposes, we will frame trauma in a very specific way. Trauma, from the Greek "to wound," is a scar, a mark that remains on our personal and collective soul. Trauma is usually seen as a fixed experience. It's something that has occurred, something over which we have no control. However, trauma is best articulated as the past recurring in the present. Rather than something that happened, it is something that is continuing to happen. Trauma is re-experienced in our memories, which is, to a large degree, separate from the historical event we are remembering.

"Past trauma" is really a misnomer. The event may have occurred in the past, but the wounding is still happening. It gets poked and prodded when we encounter events or rhetoric that reignite these "past" traumas.

Philosopher Sara Kofman's articulation at the beginning of this section—of her father's death as directly related to his Jewish identity—shows the symbiotic relationship between identity and trauma. The trauma of her father's passing is greatly intensified by her awareness that his death and his identity as a Jew are inseparable. Palestinians experience their oppression in a very similar manner. They do not see themselves as Palestinians who are persecuted, but rather that they are persecuted because they are Palestinian. This interrelationship plays out in how Jews and Palestinians resist each other, as their identities and experiences of trauma are so closely linked.

Identity—how we see ourselves—can be quite complex. For example, the Jewish identity as the victim has remained when the victimization, largely, has not. As Sara Kofman states, embedded in the Jewish experience of being maligned, oppressed, and even killed is the idea that it happened "because we are Jewish." Today, in Israel, Jews have assumed the power position, oppressing Palestinians because they see them as a threat, not unlike the way Jews were perceived in Europe. We argue that this role reversal has not only inflicted obvious harm on Palestinians but is itself a wound (trauma) to the Jewish psyche, particularly in North America, caused by the inherent tension in being both victim and victimizer.

As we discuss specific "bricks" in the wall, places where "our" truth so totally overwhelms "theirs" in the conversation about the struggle (antisemitism, Zionism and the Nakba, and Palestinian resistance), our past wounds are at work behind the scenes, never totally removed from our discourse.

Perhaps the most significant thread tying Jews and Palestinians together are "past wounds" (though, as we have discussed, they are never really "past"). While both groups endured significantly different experiences, both were marked by periods of isolation, oppression, displacement, and death. Collective memory magnifies the significance and level of pain created by the past. While connecting us within our tribe, this can also make it more difficult for many to engage in the pain of the Other. Though comparisons of suffering are never productive, understanding the shared effects of these wounds can open us up to a new appreciation for the Other and the Other's pain.

These wounds also play a role in how we imagine our future. Historical pain (the Holocaust for Jews and the Nakba for Palestinians) is not only a constant reminder of what happened, but it is seen as an indicator of what could happen in the future. For most Jews, a secure Jewish state in Israel is the only viable buffer from the return of trauma in the form of another Holocaust. For most Palestinians, freedom, self-determination, recognition of and reparations for the dispossessions of the past are the only protections from repeating the abuses of the past and addressing the abuses of the present.

These two overarching narratives of the Holocaust and the Nakba are not just historical wounds; they are still at work in the present. For Jews, it is the fear of recurrence that is most significant, whereas for Palestinians it is pain that persists day by day. The events of 1948 are not just memories of the past for Palestinians, but a lingering presence that continues to beat them down. This makes attempts at healing the trauma all the more difficult.

The need to seek confirming knowledge has created a wedge between the two groups. This wedge becomes a chasm as many have retreated into their tribal belonging. The intense trauma Palestinians and Jews have experienced deepens this divide even further, as we coalesce within our group, both to heal and to resist further trauma. However, there is another layer that may be the hardest to overcome: victimhood.

VICTIMHOOD

"The victim stance is a powerful one: The victim is always morally right, neither responsible nor accountable, and forever entitled to sympathy."
—Ofer Zur[10]

Both Jews and Palestinians view themselves as the ultimate victims and hence suffer from victimhood. We need to distinguish victimhood from victimization, or the act of being victimized. We can all identify events in our lives when we were treated unfairly or were "victimized," either individually or collectively. In contrast, victimhood is the psychological and social impact that comes from traumatizing experiences that have shaped how we see ourselves and our tribe within the broader society. Victimhood is much larger than individual events of victimization. It is the stories from these events that have left a permanent impression on us. Long-term victimhood, which has been and continues to be experienced by both Jews and Palestinians, can create the unshakable belief that what has happened to us will happen again, that there is a force that will victimize us over and over, and that our fate is predetermined unless we rise up against it and beat down those who would hurt us.

Because we are wounded by how the pain of past events resides in our present existence, our tendency towards victimhood naturally ensures that this pain will continue forever. Crucially, new wounds, like antisemitic events for Jews, or military attacks on Gaza for Palestinians, intensify old wounds while also creating new ones. It happened, it is happening again, and we are convinced it will happen in the future.

Our "victim beliefs" are a product of this re-wounding. They hit us again and again. They deplete our psychological immune system, making it susceptible to unreasonable fears of the threat posed by the Other, or how we take in information about the Other. In the case of Jews and Palestinians, victimhood has become a competition, with each victimized group insisting that they are the greater victims, oblivious to the other's victimhood.

THE BRICKS IN THE WALL

We have looked in this chapter at how identity, trauma, and victimhood (the long-term effects of grief and loss) play a primary role in the tension between "us" and "them."

While there are similarities between how Jews and Palestinians resist the other, how this manifests in the discourse in the Diasporas is strikingly different. The pro-Israel lobby has amassed such power and influence that the Jewish voice has traditionally been presented with force and prestige—as muscular. At the same time, the Palestinian voice has traditionally appeared as flailing and seemingly hopeless by comparison, although this started changing in the spring of 2021 with the inclusion of the Palestinian cause within the justice movement rising from Black Lives Matter, #MeToo, etc. Each of these voices has worked to reinforce the other.

In Part I, we have looked at the cognitive science behind why and how we tribalize. A move away from truth and reality has been happening in the world for some time. In the United States, many of us see this as a "Trump phenomenon," but it was happening long before his presidency and in many other parts of the world. It is easy to sit back and be gobsmacked that this has happened, wringing our hands at how people can be so resistant to basic truths, but this is a naive position. Our understanding of the brain—how we learn—shows us that this is the natural path humankind will choose, if it is not intentionally resisted.

In the Israel-Palestine discourse in North America, many have become immune to basic truths and created realities that fit with their own preconceptions. The "justice moment" we are in requires us to shake out of this tribal trance and reach beyond ourselves and our groups. The next part of the book will explore the "bricks in the wall," the competing narratives around antisemitism, Zionism and the Nakba, and Palestinian resistance, which have formed out of our natural resistance to seeing outside ourselves. We shouldn't be surprised that this has happened, but we need to grapple with how Jews, Palestinians, and other stakeholders have become resistant to any narrative outside of their own.

PART II – THE BRICKS IN THE WALL: COMPETING NARRATIVES

CHAPTER 4
ANTISEMITISM

"...you can't handle the truth"
(From the film *A Few Good Men*, screenplay by Aaron Sorkin)

"There's something especially unsettling about the newest eruption of the oldest hatred. Anti-Semitism has been so routine and enduring a part of human history that it's easy to become almost numb to fresh instances of it."
—Gerard Baker, *The Wall Street Journal*, May 2021[11]

Antisemitism, Antisemitism, Antisemitism

It's been with us for centuries and, some say, millennia: hatred of Jews for who they are. From European to North American societies, it enabled discrimination, marginalization, stigmatization, and victimization of entire Jewish communities.

The roots of antisemitism are multifaceted, much of it originating from the development of Christian theology where Jews were seen as responsible for killing Jesus. This religion-centered antisemitism spawned other forms of Jew-hatred during medieval times, including stereotypes of greedy Jewish businessmen and of Jews as baby killers, known as the blood libel, a centuries-old talking point against Jews that has been promoted in a variety of antisemitic propaganda literature. The faith-based roots of antisemitism were in fact driven by theo-politics, where having an Other was the surest way to cement a group within a certain set of Christian ideological teachings. Jews continued to suffer ongoing persecution, including during the Crusades, the Spanish Inquisition, the pogroms in Eastern Europe and Russia, and, of course, the Holocaust, with the residual trauma continuing to permeate the Jewish psyche in Israel and throughout the Diaspora. It was and remains one of the ugliest forms of discrimination and hate. (For more on this subject, see *Constantine's Sword* by James Carroll or *The War Against the Jews* by Lucie Dawidowicz.)

Our work in this chapter is to show how each side reacts to the discussion of antisemitism and to build a framework for understanding the Other.

It is important to note that antisemitism did not historically exist in the Middle East the way it did in Europe. In Arab lands, Jews lived alongside Muslims, Christians, and many other minorities who had settled in and around the Holy Land. (There were periodic isolated incidents of antisemitism in the Middle East, including the 1840 pogrom in Damascus, Syria, related to the medieval idea of the blood libel. For more on this, read *The Damascus Affair: Ritual Murder, Politics, and the Jews* by Jonathan Frankel.)

However, in the late nineteenth century, this generally peaceful coexistence began to weaken. The arrival of the first wave of Eastern European Jewish migration to Palestine, primarily escaping the pogroms of Russia, led to some friction between them and the Arab population. And, as Jewish migration continued in smaller numbers over the early part of the twentieth century, this friction would occasionally erupt in small-scale violence.

These acts of violence, usually followed by severe retaliation from the other side, began the cycle of resistance and resentment that continues to play out to this day. For Jews, this was yet another example of historic persecution. For Palestinian Arabs, these clashes served to instill in them a determination to repel what they saw as a colonial invasion.

This is not surprising, given what happened to the Arab nationalist dream of self-determination following the collapse of the Ottoman Empire in 1919. Having been promised independence by the British in return for their rebellion against the Ottomans during World War I, the Arabs were enraged by the publication in 1916 of the Sykes-Picot Agreement between Britain and France (and marginally, Russia) to divvy up Arab lands between the two great powers. The British and French mandates, colonial rule by another name, would end up carving Arab lands into separate colonies that mark today's borders between several Arab countries.

To Palestinian Arabs (both Christian and Muslim), the influx of European Jews into their homeland seemed a plot to replace one departing European group (British colonial rule, which lasted until 1948) with another. The Europeans, the way the Palestinians saw it, were "exiting through the door and coming right back in through the window."

In 1917, Lord Balfour of Great Britain issued the now-infamous Balfour Declaration, announcing support for the establishment of a "national home for the Jewish people" in Palestine, then an Ottoman region with a small-minority Jewish population. It reads as follows:

Foreign Office
November 2nd, 1917

Dear Lord Rothschild,

I have much pleasure in conveying to you, on behalf of His Majesty's Government, the following declaration of sympathy with Jewish Zionist aspirations which has been submitted to, and approved by, the Cabinet.

His Majesty's Government view with favour the establishment in Palestine of a national home for the Jewish people, and will use their best endeavours to facilitate the achievement of this object, it being clearly understood that nothing shall be done which may prejudice the civil and religious rights of existing non-Jewish communities in Palestine or the rights and political status enjoyed by Jews in any other country.

I should be grateful if you would bring this declaration to the knowledge of the Zionist Federation.

Yours,
Arthur James Balfour

While the Jewish nationalist movement (Zionism) was beginning to see the potential for self-realization in Palestine, Arab nationalism, the desire for self-determination, was also beginning to take root following the collapse of the Ottoman Empire. Continuous Jewish immigration and British colonial rule led to the 1936–1939 Arab revolt in Palestine, the first sustained nationalist movement among Palestinian Arabs. As it happened, the two nationalist movements were in the process of pursuing self-determination for their peoples, over the same land, at the same time. (For more on this topic, see *The Israeli/Palestinian Conflict: Contested Histories (Contesting the Past)* by Neil Caplan.) Those who see Zionism as a settler-colonial project rather than a nationalist one dispute this point.

War erupted. The large-scale migration of European Jews to Palestine following World War II, and the subsequent UN Partition Plan, dividing Palestine into two states, one Arab Palestinian and one Jewish, was followed by the 1948 Declaration of Independence of the State of Israel. The Zionist leadership accepted the UN partition plan but the Palestinians, and some Arab States, rejected it. Arab armies attacked in support of the Palestinians and the rest, as they say, is history.

The end result of these momentous events was a new political and existential reality for the two peoples: a state and a home for the Jews; displacement, dispossession, and the destruction of their society for the Palestinians.

To Jews, the new State of Israel was a fulfillment of the Zionist dream of self-determination and a historic quest for security. It came at the expense of Palestinians who, having played no part in the Holocaust, felt they had become another victim of it.

The new state of affairs between Jews and Arab Palestinians exacerbated the enmity between them, fueled by a clash over land and identity that, over time, took on racial and religious overtones. Due to the conflict and its politics, antisemitism and anti-Arab sentiment were introduced into the region, and, eventually, led to hate on both sides.

In time, an Arab, to a Jew, became "the one who wants to kill me," and a Jew, to an Arab, became "the one who wants to dispossess me." Jews saw Israel as a victim of Arab aggression aiming to wipe it out (a second Holocaust)—the Jewish David facing the Arab Goliath. Arabs saw Israel as the regional bully, aiming no less than to reclaim the ancient land of Greater Israel that stretched from the Nile to the Euphrates (Egypt to Iraq)—a hostile Western implant with imperial aims and devious ambitions.

These narratives have permeated the region for decades and continue to this day. Not surprisingly, the same narratives have made their way to the respective diasporas, along with the requisite stereotypes, prejudices, animosities, acrimonies—and the racist tropes: the violent Arab, the all-powerful Jew, among others.

Here in the West, where many are actively engaged in countering racism (including antisemitism, and Islamophobia) and promoting inclusion, these racial undertones take different turns: the mention of "antisemitism" elicits powerful yet directly opposite reactions between Jews and Palestinians.

To a Jew, antisemitism is a past trauma, a present trauma, and an almost-guaranteed future trauma. Antisemitism is a thread that runs through the tapestry of Jewish life. It is ever-present, foreboding, and certain. It weaves its way, often surreptitiously and silently through even the happiest of times. It is the monster whose haunting presence breathes down one's neck, refusing to allow any Jew to forget its existence.

To a Palestinian, antisemitism is a muzzle, a weapon to silence, defend, and deflect from or otherwise discredit critics of Israel's actions. It is a club to clobber the heads of those taking a stand for Palestine, and the shackle that ties down the hands of solidarity. It is the boot that presses down one's neck, choking speech, silencing thought, removing voice, and eliminating hope. It's an "occupation" of the narrative.

Antisemitism is this powerful force that, in effect, ends up oppressing both Jews and Palestinians.

Likewise, the Star of David, a symbol once used to oppress Jews, is now not only a ubiquitous representative symbol of the Jewish people and the Jewish state, it is also emblazoned on Israeli tanks and the wings of fighter jets that bomb Palestinians—freedom for one, oppression for another.

Yet it is necessary to review the different lenses through which Jews and Palestinians view the conflict between them. The reasons for our unique reactions to antisemitism, we argue, are rooted in how our identity, trauma and victimhood are at work, on a social and psychological level, in both Jews and Palestinians. This is also true in Western society as a whole, where our response to the two narratives is framed largely on who we see as part of "us" and who is part of "them."

From a trauma lens, Jews view Israel as the ultimate weapon defending against the scourge of antisemitism—and even the threat of a second Holocaust—and, therefore, everything connected to Israel is connected to antisemitism. When a mention of Israel is made, it is processed through the filter of antisemitism, and, due to historic trauma, the intent of it is assumed to be antisemitic, until proven otherwise. Israel is about survival.

A natural question for Jews is that if Israel had existed in 1933, would the Nazis have been able to commit the genocide of the Shoah? Many, such as Eve Spangler in her 2015 book *Understanding Israel/Palestine: Race, Nation, and Human Rights* have asked, had there been F-15s flying over Auschwitz, could the mass murder of Jews have occurred? Given the workings of trauma and victimhood, the line between Zionism and the Holocaust can never be underestimated. The Holocaust is a narrative woven into the very nature of what it means to be Jewish, and Israel, as a representation of Jewish liberation and self-determination at the psycho-traumatic level, is viewed as the only buffer from Jewish annihilation.

While many Jews make a clear distinction between antisemitism and criticism of Israel, these deeply held connections to the state of Israel and its representation of Jewish protection naturally bubble up when Israel is criticized, making the charge of antisemitism erupt from the Jewish psyche almost involuntarily.

To a Palestinian, Israel is the ultimate usurper of land and identity. It has been taking over historic Palestine, piece by piece by piece. In 1948, 78 percent of Palestine[12] became Israel. After 1967, settlements were built and land appropriated in the West Bank. There was annexation and Judaization of East Jerusalem, the wall that carves deep into occupied territory was built, and claims have been made over the Jordan Valley—all told, revealing an insatiable appetite for Palestinian land. The seemingly endless oppression of the occupation only adds salt to an already-festering wound. Trauma is, in part, the grieving of what has been lost. Israel is about loss.

Antisemitism, Antisemitism, Antisemitism

When we hear the word "antisemitism" here in North America and in Europe, we immediately think of the Holocaust, its ultimate and most unspeakable expression. We all do, even the Palestinians among us, thanks to the highly effective and sustained efforts of education about the Holocaust and its commemoration that keep the memory alive in all of us.

To a Jew, the trauma and the enormity of the Holocaust remain ingrained with such urgency that it is part of the past, the present, and the future: it happened once, and it can—likely will—happen again. (That being said, projects to memorialize the Holocaust didn't start in earnest until the late 1960s and have proliferated in the years since. There was a "delayed impact," as Franklin Bialystok's *Delayed Impact: The Holocaust and the Canadian Jewish Community* shows). A long history of oppression and antisemitism supports this view. It is essential therefore to prevent a recurrence by defending Israel and ensuring its survival—no matter what. It's a matter of life and death. Jews have paid enough throughout their history and shouldn't have to pay anymore. No matter what.

To a Palestinian, the Holocaust and antisemitism are something completely different: they are the originators and enablers of Jewish exceptionalism. Sympathy for Jews among Western nations following World War II, along with their guilt for having denied entry to Jewish migrants fleeing the Nazis during the war, is what allowed the creation of the State of Israel on Palestinian land. Some Arab intellectuals and political thinkers share the belief that Western countries supported the creation of a Jewish state in the Middle East partly to preserve Western influence in a strategically important region. For Palestinians, sympathy for past Jewish suffering is used as a means to justify the Occupation, settlements, and even the killing of Palestinians. This too is trauma in action. As Jews connect antisemitism to the Holocaust, Palestinians see this connection as the rationale for 1948, for 1967, and for the ongoing Occupation. The use of antisemitism, in the mind of many Palestinians, to excuse or explain why Jews deserve the land of Palestine/Israel, at their expense, is a re-wounding of the trauma, specifically of the Nakba.

To a Jew, patterns of antisemitism are visible in many places—not just among racist individuals and white-supremacist types but also among governments, multilateral institutions, and societies in Europe and the Arab countries. The UN is seen as inherently biased against Israel and, therefore, against Jews. This is evidenced by what many Jews see as a disproportionate number of anti-Israel resolutions at the UN General Assembly and UN Human Rights Council; between 1975 and 1991, for example, United Nations General Assembly resolution 3379, which equated Zionism with racism, was in effect. Why do they target Israel, if it's not for antisemitism? Discrimination is self-evident in any disproportionate treatment.

A Palestinian, in turn, would point out that it was the UN General Assembly that created Israel, and the US-assured veto at the UN Security Council in support of Israel, proves the body is lopsided in favor of Israel. For Palestinians, the constant criticism of the UN General Assembly, including by the United States government that consistently votes against these resolutions, is another example of the pro-Israel lobby using its considerable clout to silence even this internationally sanctioned form of pushback—mainstreamed muscularity versus marginalized resistance, once again.

A nuance that is important here is that the UN is responsible for creating the partition plan, officially recognizing the State of Israel through the passage of Resolution 180 on November 29, 1947, by a vote of 33 - 13. What some may consider the UN's outsized interest in Israel stems largely from the fact that it sees itself as responsible for the formation of and legitimization of the state and also for its many consequences on Arab Palestinians.

American, Canadian, and most Western governments have, to a large degree, chosen a side to support and one to diminish. Our discussion on antisemitism is framed within the understanding that the body politic in North America generally aligns itself with the Jewish-Israeli narrative and sees Palestinian Arabs as outsiders, even dangerous.

A constant sticking point between many Jews and Palestinians is the Boycott, Divestment, and Sanctions movement (BDS), started in 2005 "to end international support for Israel's oppression of Palestinians and pressure Israel to comply with international law." It was a call by Palestinian civil society, inspired by the South African anti-apartheid movement, urging "nonviolent pressure on Israel until it complies with international law" by meeting three demands: an end to the occupation, equal rights for Arab Palestinian citizens of Israel, and a right of return to Palestinian refugees to their homes in Israel.

To a Jew who identifies with Israel as a matter of personal survival, BDS looks nothing short of an attempt to delegitimize and isolate Israel. BDS also brings up historical memories of Jewish businesses being boycotted in Europe at various times, including in the years leading up to the Holocaust. The campaign in support of BDS presents the struggle between Israel and the Palestinians as the fault of only one party: Israel. And by calling for the right of return of Palestinian refugees of 1948 and their descendants to present-day Israel, the sole aim can only be to destroy the State of Israel as a Jewish-majority state. Therefore, how can BDS be anything but antisemitic, yet another symbol of Jewish re-victimization?

"They are out to get us." The "they" has changed, but the feelings have not.

To a Palestinian, this looks like yet another attempt to silence and crush any criticism of Israel, using antisemitism as a club. If a Palestinian is unable to even participate in a nonviolent effort of resistance against Israel's occupation without being called a racist, what else is left to do? Supporters of Israel can only be looking to silence a debate they know they can't win.

To a Palestinian, BDS has nothing to do with antisemitism. To a Jew, it has everything to do with it.

Antisemitism, Antisemitism, Antisemitism

The latest battle in the war of defining what is or isn't antisemitism, or who is or isn't a Jew-hater, came in the form of a working definition of antisemitism conceived in 2016 by the International Holocaust Remembrance Alliance (IHRA). Founded in 1998, the IHRA is an intergovernmental organization mandated to focus on Holocaust-related issues. It has 32 member countries, mostly in Europe and North America. The IHRA definition, which has been adopted by many governments and other institutions across the globe, states:

> "Antisemitism is a certain perception of Jews, which may be expressed as hatred toward Jews. Rhetorical and physical manifestations of antisemitism are directed toward Jewish or non-Jewish individuals and/or their property, toward Jewish community institutions and religious facilities."

It is important to understand the genesis and implementation of the working definition of antisemitism. At the American Jewish Committee

(1989-2014), lawyer and an academic Kenneth Stern spearheaded the effort to draft a working definition of antisemitism, with eleven illustrative examples as key components. The committee's primary purpose was to provide European data collectors tasked with creating reports on antisemitism guidelines of what to include, as well as to give guidance on hate crime analysis (looking at the intent to select a target because it was Jewish or linked to Jews, rather than questions of motive). The EUMC took the definition on board as a "working definition," but never officially adopted it. The IHRA adopted it in 2016, and it was this placing of the definition within IHRA that has led to how the working definition is operationalized today. Framing it within the context of Holocaust remembrance tied the history of Jewish victimization to the need for Israel. Jewish trauma and feelings of victimhood are directly ensconced in the working definition.

Seven of the eleven illustrative examples mention Israel, such as one that refers to "applying double standards by requiring of [Israel] a behavior not expected or demanded of any other democratic nation."

In each of the examples referring to criticism of Israel or differential treatment of Israel, it aligns with the goal of protecting Israel, and thereby protecting Jews, yet it lands very differently for Palestinians. Given that Israel is unique among democratic nations in that it continues to occupy (some say colonize) another people, for a Palestinian, Israel is not being treated differently because it is a Jewish state, but rather because it is an occupying power.

For instance, if a Palestinian were to object to Israel's use of snipers against mostly civilian demonstrators gathered near Gaza's borders with Israel during the March of Return in 2019, that person might be accused of antisemitism on the basis that any democratic nation can be expected to protect its border (as Israel has said it was doing). For a Palestinian, the trauma of soldiers shooting at unarmed protesters is greatly exacerbated by the use of the IHRA definition to silence criticism of that action.

It is reasonable for a group that feels threatened or oppressed to want to describe and articulate their oppression. However, in the context of Jewish/Palestinian power dynamics, the pervasive acceptance of this definition, including the many examples referring to Israel, makes this less straightforward than one might think. We are now in a place where, if even a small municipality is hesitant to adopt the IHRA definition, it is labeled antisemitic and subjected to an online barrage of accusations. Similarly, all governments that adopt the definition are hailed as protectors of universal human rights.

To a Palestinian, the real purpose of the IHRA definition is not to educate about and create a universally understood definition of antisemitism, but rather to protect Israel from its critics—ensuring that the oppression of Palestinians continues. A Palestinian sees Israel as a nuclear power with a large and ultra-modern army, a thriving economy, and the unyielding support of the United States, and can't understand why it needs protection from criticism.

To a Jew, IHRA is protection. To a Palestinian, it is oppression. This is more than a different perspective; this is our wounds barking at us, warning each of us that we are under attack from the Other.

If adopted by governments and institutions (even though these adoptions are not legally binding), as many Jewish organizations in the West have been advocating for their governments to do, IHRA could make expressions in support of Palestinian rights, against Israel's occupation, or criticizing Israel's treatment of the Palestinians a perilous endeavor. For Palestinians, a group that already feels they have very limited means of redress for their difficulties, the politically powerful pro-Israel lobby's accusations of antisemitism only increase their sense of hopelessness and fuels the need to resist.

On August 3, 2019, British newspaper *The Guardian* reported a story about a town council in London refusing to give a license to The Big Ride for Palestine—an annual event that raises funds to buy sports equipment for the children of Gaza—"over antisemitism fears." Finding strong criticism of Israel on the organizers' website (including comparisons to apartheid-era South Africa and accusations of ethnic cleansing), the town council feared the event and its organizers would be in breach of the IHRA definition. As a result, there was no Big Ride for Palestine, and no sports equipment for the children of Gaza.

To a Palestinian, the challenge of the IHRA definition is that the many examples relating to Israel create the impression that any criticism of Israel can be labeled antisemitic. As a result, decision-makers are more likely to err on the side of caution and avoid or ban an activity rather than risk being seen as tolerating antisemitism. The goal of the Big Ride—getting much-needed sports equipment to the children of Gaza—is overwhelmed by the fear of looking antisemitic. This perpetuates the story of Jewish muscularity and entrenches the view of Palestinian resistance as flailing and unproductive.

In May 2019, the *Bundestag* (the German lower house of parliament) passed a non-binding resolution that stated "the pattern of argument and methods of the BDS movement are anti-Semitic," and called on the government not to financially support any projects that call for the boycott of Israel, or actively support the BDS campaign.[13] This led to a series of McCarthy-esque efforts to discredit once highly regarded academics and leaders of cultural institutions, to the point where these academics and leaders came together to push back strongly in a united act against silencing freedom of expression.

This resolution in Germany is, in part, a response to the societal trauma caused by the Holocaust on the German people, the rise in far-right antisemitic incidents in Germany in the previous few years, and the incredible effectiveness of the pro-Israel lobby in capitalizing on these fissures in German society. It is important to understand that these types of resolutions that seek to silence critics of Israel, thereby protecting Jews, are often counterproductive, causing a rise in anti-Jewish sentiment rather than diminishing it.

The reality is the concept of "new antisemitism," which equates anti-Zionism with antisemitism and is alluded to in the IHRA definition, conflates Israel with Judaism and Judaism with Israel to the point where the line between the two is blurred for everyone involved. In one of the IHRA definition's illustrative examples, denying the Jewish people the right to self-determination is considered antisemitic—implying a connection between merely questioning the right to self-determination and anti-Zionism.

Antisemitism, Antisemitism, Antisemitism

The filter in search of antisemitic intent that is present in the head, guts, and heart of many Jews often goes into overdrive. It's a 24-7 alert system for the recurrence of antisemitism. This is how trauma works in the present, though its source, at least in part, is in the past. The fear of antisemitism and the trauma and victimhood it evokes is a major obstacle for many Jews who are dedicated to justice for Palestinians.

One prominent example is the case of US Representative Ilhan Omar, one of the first two Muslim women elected to Congress, in 2018. Omar created a political and media storm in February 2019 as she entered into the world of antisemitic tropes—three times in a row. First, quoting a line about $100 bills from a Puff Daddy song, she invoked the role of "Benjamins" in silencing criticism of Israel; then she accused the American Israel Public Affairs Committee (AIPAC) of funding Republican support for Israel; and lastly, in a speech, she asked why "it is OK for people to push for allegiance to a foreign country?"—meaning Israel.

Buying influence, controlling politicians, and having dual loyalty to a foreign country are all often-repeated antisemitic tropes, practiced by the likes of modern white supremacists like David Duke and reaching back to medieval representations of the menacing, conniving Jew, filled with self-interest and contempt for Christian society. Omar clearly needed an education about such tropes and acknowledged as much in her public apology. But she remained steadfast in her point about money influencing politics in the US, citing, in addition to AIPAC, the National Rifle Association (NRA) and fossil fuel lobbies.

The attacks on Omar were relentless and from many sides, including from her own party and Speaker of the House Nancy Pelosi. House Democrats voted overwhelmingly in support of a resolution condemning antisemitism that read as a clear rebuke of Omar personally, criticizing the "insidious, bigoted history" of "accusations of dual loyalty." A website called StopAntsemitism.org voted Ilhan Omar its "Anti-Semite of the Year,"[14] and she became the target of vicious

Islamophobic language and xenophobic threats from anonymous senders as well as from the White House and the halls of Congress.

Could Ilhan Omar have made her point without using antisemitic tropes? Certainly. But the rookie congresswoman wasn't given the benefit of the doubt. Once someone like Congresswoman Omar is labeled an antisemite, nothing else she says on the subject is listened to, including her reasonable criticism of the influence of AIPAC in American politics as well as just criticism of America's Israel policy.

Is Ilhan Omar an anti-Semite? Your predisposition on the subject will likely determine the answer.

We saw firsthand evidence of honest, well-meaning, and peace-seeking Jews who were deeply hurt by what she said. These were progressive individuals who had been delighted to see a young, Black, hijab-wearing Muslim woman make it to Congress. They were people who were critical of many Israeli policies and openly expressed their opposition to them. Yet trauma was reignited by the sound of antisemitic tropes coming out of her mouth, leaving no room for a rational and thorough investigation into the person or the motivations behind her comments.

Without the presence of trauma and victimhood, one may conclude that Ilhan Omar misspoke, that she was in need of education about antisemitic tropes, but likely will not jump to the conclusion that she was inherently antisemitic herself, for lack of evidence.

The Omar incident shows the perils of speaking out against Israel, given the abundance of opportunity to fall into antisemitic tropes. Trauma trumps rationale.

The following year, Honest Reporting, a US-based organization dedicating itself to "defending Israel against media bias," published an article[15] titled "How to Criticize Israel Without Being Antisemitic," listing ten things to remember for "people who want to fairly criticize Israel without falling into antisemitic canards or tropes."

While aiming to be helpful, some of the list's suggestions, such as "make a fair attempt to understand Israeli policies" and "speak from a place of knowledge, accuracy and context," belong in an introductory guide to journalism. Which is all well, but what if you don't follow such rules? You might fail in journalism, but are you necessarily antisemitic? According to the article, you are. The suggestion is that certain rules apply only to journalism about Israel. Dealing with Israel—its policies, actions, and potential crimes and misdemeanors—is different from dealing with any other state. Because of antisemitism.

In November 2018, CNN commentator and Temple University professor Marc Lamont Hill delivered a speech[16] at the United Nations on the occasion of the International Day of Solidarity With the Palestinian People. After speaking in support of Palestinian self-determination and equal rights, he concluded by saying, "We have an opportunity to not just offer solidarity in words, but to commit to ... action that will give us what justice requires, and that is a free Palestine, from the river to the sea."

Less than twenty-four hours later, he was fired by CNN. He was let go because of his use of the words "from the river to the sea," in reference to the territory of historic Palestine, situated between the Jordan River and the Mediterranean Sea prior to the creation of Israel in 1948. The reference was deemed antisemitic, as it seemed to challenge the very existence of Jews in the land. However, Lamont Hill was not speaking of removing Jews, but advocating for freedom for all the people, Jews and Palestinians, living in historic Palestine. This highlights the differences between how many Jews and Palestinians see the notion of "the river to the sea." For most Palestinians, it is not about challenging the existence of Jews in the land, but rather creating equal rights and opportunities for all Palestinians between "the river and the sea."

To a Palestinian supporter, the road to antisemitism appears to be wide, slippery, and under perpetual, intentional reconstruction.

For Jews, the IHRA definition is a welcome tool in the fight against antisemitism. While many Jews may object to the Occupation and the settlements in the West Bank, they are concerned that anti-Israel sentiment is linked, in some cases, with antisemitism. The issue here is the impact of governments and other institutions adopting the IHRA definition to silence Palestinians, further cementing the "wall" between. While many Jews see IHRA as a positive force, the impact on Palestinian rights and expression does not enter into the formula. Kenneth Stern, defended the right of free speech. In one opinion piece[6] in 2019, he explained that the original intent of the working definition was "so that European data collectors could know what to include and exclude. That way antisemitism could be monitored better over time and across borders."

Stern states, "Starting in 2010, right-wing Jewish groups took the 'working definition,' which had some examples about Israel ... and decided to weaponize it," by pressuring lawmakers to enshrine it into law, which, in the U.S., took effect in the form of an executive order by the Trump administration. Stern discerns that "the real purpose of the executive order isn't to tip the scales in a few Title VI cases,[17] but rather the chilling effect" on pro-Palestinian speech.

A Palestinian sees that "antisemitism" has been overused, misused, and abused. Jewish organizations have diluted the meaning of antisemitism and made the charge such common and easy currency that others now use it for their own purposes.

In August 2019, President Trump told reporters,[18] "In my opinion, the Democrats have gone very far away from Israel ... You vote for a Democrat, you're being very disloyal to Jewish people and you're being very disloyal to Israel," thereby accusing Jewish Democrats of being antisemitic. Later that same year, right-wing circles used the antisemitism charge to discredit Senator Bernie Sanders—a Jewish left-wing Democrat who had spent time on a kibbutz in Israel and was running for the Democratic presidential nomination.[19] Writing in the *Washington Examiner* in December 2019, conservative columnist Tiana Lowe accused the Sanders campaign of being "the most anti-Semitic in decades."[20]

In Canada, respected Jewish community leaders who had dedicated their lives to fighting antisemitism were called antisemitic by people in their community for supporting the Liberal Party (instead of the ultra-Israel-friendly Conservative Party) in the 2011 federal election.

By labeling BDS antisemitic, Palestinian supporters saw supporters of Israel being handed a new big stick to further beat them down with.

In 2017, the State of Texas passed legislation that prohibits state agencies from investing in companies that boycott Israel or giving them government contracts. With bipartisan support, it passed unanimously in the House and with little opposition in the Senate. Texas is one of over two dozen (mostly Republican-led) states that have taken such action in response to the BDS call. The legislation requires anyone signing a contract with a state agency (such as public schools and universities) to sign a pledge that they would not participate in the boycott of Israel.

In April 2019, US District Judge Robert Pitman issued a temporary injunction on the Texas law, siding with Palestinian speech pathologist Bahia Amawi, who had lost her contract position with the Pflugerville School district. Amawi refused to sign an agreement saying she does not and will not boycott Israel for the remainder of her contract. She told the court that "Israel has long mistreated her family and other Palestinians and she could not in good conscience certify that she would refuse to boycott the country."[21]

The judge ruled that the law "violates the First Amendment's protection against government intrusion into political speech and expression." The American Civil Liberties Union, an intervenor in the case, reacted that "the right to boycott is deeply ingrained in American tradition, from our nation's founding to today. The state cannot dictate the views of its own citizens on the Israel-Palestine conflict—or any issue—by preventing them from exercising their First Amendment right to boycott."[22]

The Guardian ran a story in October 2019 about a conservative network known as a "bill mill," which debates and propagates right-wing policies at the state level through "model" bills. The article described the group's efforts to suppress criticism of Israel on US campuses.[23] The story came out of a conference in August held by the American Legislative Exchange Council, where a private meeting took place that included a number of state lawmakers led by Randy Fine, a Republican from Florida, who was instrumental in passing that state's first state law outlawing antisemitism in public education. Email exchanges following the meeting made clear the motive behind the push for antisemitism-on-campus bills was countering criticism of Israel. In one email, Fine wrote that under the new laws "Antisemitism (whether acts by students, administrators or faculty, policies and procedures, club organizations, etc.) [will] be treated identically to how racism is treated. Students for Justice in Palestine are now treated the same way as the Ku Klux Klan—as they should be."

Ironically, such weaponization of antisemitism to silence support for Palestinian rights can only create hate and/or resentment towards Jews among Palestinian supporters. And those who are truly defending against antisemitism are done no favor by equating supporters of Palestinian rights with white supremacists.

It is important to note how Israel's right-wing governments under prime minister Benjamin Netanyahu (2009–2021, 2022– ...) intentionally fostered close relations with nationalist governments in Eastern Europe that have a history of embedded antisemitism. Additionally, it had no issues with the Trump administration, which, while being the most pro-Israel in US history, has shown softness towards white supremacists and engaged in antisemitic tropes on a number of occasions.[24] Also, we need to look critically at the alliance between the American Jewish lobby and Evangelical Christian Zionists whose ultimate goal is for the Messiah to return to Israel and for the Jews there to convert to Christianity. They appear to be pro-Israel while holding on to vestiges of religious-based antisemitism.

What we are illuminating here is that you can be both pro-Israel and antisemitic. Conversely, you can be deeply critical of Israel, and even of Zionism, and not be antisemitic. The pro-Israel lobby, when trying to silence the BDS movement on college and university campuses by labeling it antisemitic, has consequently engendered fear in Jewish students. These students began feeling threatened when encountering BDS supporters, while most of these supporters were out to show solidarity with Palestinian rights and not to target other students. We agree there have been occasional incidents where Jewish students were harassed over their perceived views on Israel, however, we argue that by linking BDS and antisemitism, a heightened sense of danger has been created, exaggerating the threat to Jewish students on college and university campuses, and limiting the possibility of Jewish and pro-Palestinian students learning from each other. This can be directly tied to the culture of "safetyism" we referred to earlier. Unfortunately, the result is to foster fear rather than resilience in Jewish students. Being exposed to a BDS rally can be viewed as eye-opening rather than dangerous. Exposing one to the experiences of another should never be viewed as harmful, but rather as a bridge to the Other.

It has become hard, especially for a Palestinian, to suppress disbelief upon hearing the word "antisemitism." It is equally hard for a Palestinian to not feel threatened by it. We know that for saying this, we will likely be accused of antisemitism by some. This is the cycle of accusations and counter-accusations this book aims to interrupt.

What we have charted here is how the wall between, for both Jewish and Palestinian communities, and in the North American body politic, has formed over the issue of antisemitism. For many Jews, antisemitism is both a past and present reality, from stories of Holocaust recounted at the family table to memories of being taunted or beaten for being Jewish, or present-day stories of the mass murders of Jews in Pittsburgh and Poway, and violent incidents in New York City.

Malevolent stereotypes and hateful language are part of every Jewish person's experience, either personally or in stories from others in their immediate circle. The scourge of antisemitism is so embedded in Jewish religious and/or cultural identity that separating harmful language and actions from the reasonable protest against Israeli policies, which are often seen as threats to Israel's existence, is harder than we might think.

We have talked to many progressive Jews and, to a person, they make a clear distinction between criticism of Israel and antisemitism. The challenge is that "on the ground" in our day-to-day conversations, words and actions that many Palestinians and their supporters feel are reasonable criticisms, can manifest, to many, as antisemitic.

The reasons for this are varied, but they primarily seem to stem from the fear of losing Israel as a Jewish state, and thereby exposing world Jewry to discrimination and/or eventual extinction. As we have articulated, some of this stems from references that tap into old antisemitic tropes and the harm to Jews that this caused in the past. We are asking the reader to do the tough emotional work of dealing with these triggers and remaining in the conversation in spite of them.

For Palestinians, identity, trauma, and victimhood also play a large role in how many view the subject of antisemitism. We have cited many examples where antisemitism was used as a tool to silence Palestinian resistance to specific Israeli policies and actions, but there is an emotional component as well. The history of oppression of the Jews and the Holocaust has, in the eyes of many Palestinians, been used as a justification for the dispossession of their land and the ongoing hardships that are the daily reality of Palestinians in the Occupied territories. The daily reminders, in articles, media posts, in political speeches, and even in legislation, of the presence of antisemitism triggers their traumatic past and re-victimizes Palestinians by silencing them. The overwhelming message to them is, "Not only do you have to accept what we have done to you, but you can't protest our actions because of antisemitism."

In Palestinian/Jewish dialogue, a Palestinian may ask a Jewish participant, "After what was done to you, how could you do this to us?" Naturally, this is very painful for the Jewish participant to hear, and, in our experience, they strongly resist what they see as a wholly unjust comparison. We offer that this question perfectly articulates the dilemma of antisemitism in today's conversation. For a Palestinian, asking this question is central to determining why antisemitism that happened elsewhere is resolved on their backs. For a Jew, minimizing the scope and tragedy of the Holocaust by comparing it to something they view as entirely different is a case of classic antisemitism.

Our work here is to help Jews and Palestinians better understand how antisemitism is viewed by the respective tribes, and society as a whole, and to reflect on the consequences if it goes on unchecked. Both tribes are victimized by antisemitism, as it is a paralyzing force in our interactions and a giant barrier to our dreams of a just and equal society.

In explaining how differently we can perceive things like antisemitism, our intention is to challenge the notion that any of us truly sees the complete picture. All of us are limited in our ability to see the entirety of an issue. However, true justice requires us to push the limits of our perceptions. In the antisemitism debate, while we promote a more nuanced view on what is and isn't antisemitic, there is a larger goal. From a justice and human rights lens, if we are focusing on one injustice as a means of hiding another, then this is not a rights-driven, justice-based endeavor.

CHAPTER 5
ZIONISM AND THE NAKBA

"We had no other choice. After the Holocaust, we had no other choice."
"Palestine is a wonderful place. It is like a beautiful girl,
but the girl is already engaged."
—From the film *Colliding Dreams* (2015),
directed by Joseph Dorman and Oren Rudavsky

ZIONISM

"Zionism is like a person escaping a burning building, jumping out of the
window and falling on someone else's head."
—*Colliding Dreams*

Once upon a time, there was a young girl out wandering in the woods. After several terrifying ordeals—an attack by a pack of bloodthirsty wolves, a thrashing windstorm, and the crushing awareness that she was completely lost—an enticing aroma drew her towards a small cabin that appeared just when all seemed to be lost. As she opened the door, slightly taken aback by the creaking sound, she tiptoed into the cozy surroundings. She gently called out, "Anybody home?" After a few more attempts at rousing someone, she stepped towards a small table where three bowls of porridge had been left out, as if someone had just made a swift departure. She sampled each of the bowls, deciding on the one that seemed "just right," and cleaned the bowl right down to the last morsel. The walk and the warm porridge left her feeling rather exhausted, so she crept up the stairs and fell fast asleep. The little cabin suited her so well that even after the inhabitants returned, she decided that this was a perfect new home for her, a place where she could be warm, safe, and never go hungry.

Once upon a time, there was a little village that was home to three little pigs. The pigs were quite self-sufficient and had managed to live very content lives, with little concern for the dangers that surrounded them. Then, one day, a hungry wolf wandered into town. He was on the prowl for his next meal, and when he spotted the three little pigs, his mouth drooled in anticipation. "I'll huff and I'll puff and I'll blow your house down," howled the big bad wolf as he came to the first little pig's house. This little pig seemed quite unconcerned. His house was nothing more than some thatched straw, but he had made do on his wits in the past and was sure this would be no different. Sadly, he had greatly misjudged the situation and the wolf did indeed blow his house down, sending the little pig scurrying into the surrounding hills.

The second little pig had heard the commotion and began to prepare himself for the wolf's impending visit. He buttoned up his little wooden house as best he could in the limited time he had and stood proudly at the front door, assured he could dissuade the wolf from destroying his home. But alas the wolf howled again, "I'll huff and I'll puff and I'll blow your house down." The pig tried to reason with the wolf. "But Mr. Wolf, this house has been in my family for many generations, and we have cared for the land and we don't want to move away." The wolf seemed amused by the fruitless protest and proceeded to puff up his chest and let out a giant torrent of air that toppled the little home before the little pig's eyes.

Now, the third little pig had heard the stories of the big bad wolf and was determined not to suffer that same fate as his friends. Being the planning type, he had already fortified his little home with steel and concrete and knew that he was prepared for whatever the wolf could bring down on him. Seeing the third little pig standing defiantly in front of his home, the wolf gave a wry smile, a seeming nod to the pig's fiery resolve, and then howled as loud as his lungs would allow, "I'll huff and I'll puff and I'll blow your house down." He blew and he blew and he blew, but the little house and the little pig stood tall and strong. The wolf, matching the pig's willpower, summoned twenty of his wolf friends to the little house, and they blew it off the land and sent the third little pig fleeing the town as his brothers had before him.

Zionism is neither a single narrative nor a single perspective on a narrative, but rather a multitude of tales and perspectives. The Jews who emigrated to Palestine were neither the stereotype of the lost damsel or the ruthless wolf, but these narratives have been spun over time, and, depending on the benefit or loss you have experienced from the forming of Israel as a Jewish state, you will likely view Zionism starkly differently.

In a clever children's book called *The True Story of the Three Little Pigs,* author Jon Scieszka offers the story from the wolf's perspective. In this version, the wolf is a mild-mannered creature that has been given an entirely bad rap, and if we just learned to understand him better, we would feel very differently about the story of the three little pigs. We might also retell the story with the wolf being a victim of terrible tragedies himself, which led to his behavior with the pigs.

In fact, in almost every conversation about Zionism, the wolf, or in some tellings the lost damsel, are the central figures. The pigs are a side story. Zionism was envisioned and realized by Jews but inflicted on Palestinians. While we may get caught up in differentiating the various articulations of Zionism today (progressive Zionism, religious Zionism, secular Zionism, liberal Zionism, aspirational Zionism, etc.), we must deal with this fact first. Yet it is not a simple story of a perpetrator and a victim. It is a story of two groups of victims.

Zionism is both an idea and an ideal. It is about liberation for Jews. It was imagined by a small group of European Jewish men in the latter half of the nineteenth century, the most well-known being

Theodor Herzl, an Austro-Hungarian playwright and journalist. Herzl's story is a microcosm of the Jewish narrative. He lived a relatively peaceful existence in his homeland but was well aware of antisemitism. Seeking refuge from a deeply unhappy marriage, he took a job as the Paris correspondent for the Viennese newspaper *Neue Freie Presse*. He covered many stories related to the rise of antisemitism in France, culminating in the notorious Dreyfus Affair. Alfred Dreyfus was a French army captain who was accused of being a traitor. He was convicted, referred to as a Judas, and exiled. Though evidence emerged that someone else had committed the treasonous act, this was covered up, and Dreyfus was retried and convicted again, although he was later exonerated.

The Dreyfus Affair, as well as many other incidents in France and around Europe, were strong warning signals to Jews that they would always be judged first for being Jewish, with all the negative stereotypes this entailed. Herzl and many others took these events to mean that Jews would never be safe in Europe and that they must have a place of permanent refuge.

The insider-outsider status of many influential European Jews can be encapsulated by the story of Maurice de Hirsch, who helped fund Herzl's Zionist dream. Born into a wealthy Bavarian banking family in 1831, de Hirsch became extraordinarily rich through a deal with the Ottoman Empire to build a rail link between Turkey and the West, through the Balkans. He developed relationships with very important people, including the Prince of Wales, Prince Rudolf of Austria, and the president of France, who was his neighbor on the Rue de l'Élysée. The paradox to his power and wealth was that, while he could have purchased the famous Vienna Jockey Club many times over, the club blackballed him because he was a Jew. He gave away a small fortune to support Jews subjected to the pogroms in Russia and to the Zionist cause.

Those who gathered at the First Zionist Congress, held in Basel, Switzerland, in 1897, had all had experiences similar to those of de Hirsch. They had personally witnessed the limits of their own power and wealth due to their ethnic and religious origin, and, even more profoundly, had watched the rampant spread of antisemitism in Europe. While this manifested most dramatically in Russia, all of Europe now seemed susceptible to the disease of antisemitism.

As we described, metaphorically, in the differing renditions of Goldilocks and the Three Bears and The Three Little Pigs, Zionism holds multiple truths together. Was it a project designed by a fearful, historically oppressed group to create a sort of safety zone for its people? Was it a purposeful plan of colonization by a band of European, entitled white men? Was it both? The simplest answer is that there are elements of each in how Zionism was envisioned and carried out. Most importantly, your tribal perspective will largely determine your viewpoint, as in most of the discussions here. We are pushing you outside of your tribal lens—to see Zionism (and the Nakba) from another perspective.

While there are many turning points in the Zionist project, three are likely the most instructive. We have talked briefly about the First Zionist Congress in 1897. There have been, in fact, thirty-seven Zionist congresses (as of 2020) over a 120-year period. The first twenty-one meetings of congress happened almost every year until 1921. Since the founding of Israel, the congress meets every five years.

Presided over by Herzl, the first conference formally created the World Zionist Organization (WZO). Herzl proclaimed the goal of Zionism was "to seek for the Jewish people a publicly recognized, secured homeland in Palestine."

A second seminal moment was the Balfour Declaration of 1917, and the subsequent British mandate over Palestine after World War I. This gave Zionism a new legitimacy in the world. The omnipotent British Empire, at the encouragement of Chaim Weitzmann, one of the leaders of the WZO, recognized the right of Jews to form a homeland in Palestine. This first consent from a Western power set the stage for the almost-unanimous support that Israel still enjoys from the world's democracies.

The Twelfth Zionist Congress took place in Carlsbad, Czechoslovakia, in 1921, four years after the Balfour Declaration. The defeat of the Triple Alliance (Germany, Austria-Hungary, and the Ottomans)—effectively ending five hundred years of Ottoman control over historic Palestine and the entire surrounding region—and the subsequent awarding of Palestine to the British (referred to as the Palestine Mandate or the British Mandate), set in motion the creation of the State of Israel thirty-seven years later.

As was recognized by the Twelfth Congress, the situation on the ground with Palestinians was becoming a significant challenge for the Zionists. This was due in large part to a major influx of Jews in the early twentieth century, mostly escaping the pogroms in Russia, which led to the Arab uprisings in 1920 and 1921, where over 100 people died and several hundred were wounded. As a result, the congress formally stated a commitment "to live in relations of harmony and mutual respect with the Arab people" in Palestine, and called on the executive to achieve a "sincere understanding with the Arab people." However, this was never successful, and, again, who you see as primarily responsible for this failure likely rests in your general disposition on the Israel-Palestine struggle.

The British Mandate created difficulties for both Jews and Arab Palestinians in order to limit their ability to form armed resistance, and quelled attempts by both groups. However, the Jewish militias seemed to be far more successful at gathering arms and training their members than the Arabs. There continued to be periodic clashes with casualties on both sides.

THE NAKBA

"We are victims of victims and refugees of refugees."
—Edward Said, "The One State Solution," *The New York Times Magazine,* Jan. 10, 1999

As we shift here to talk about the Nakba, it is essential that a supporter of Zionism listen from the place of striving to grasp the impact of 1948 on Palestinians, to hear their trauma, not in relation to Jewish trauma but as something distinctly Palestinian. Zionism needs to be seen in its entirety, which must include its impact on Palestinians. We need to frame Zionism, as the quote from the film *Colliding Dreams* at the beginning of this chapter reminds us, not just as understanding the power of escaping the burning building, but the impact of that escape on those who were landed on.

The third and clearly most significant event in the history of Zionism was the so-called War of Independence and the Declaration of the State of Israel in May 1948. This was the culmination, at least in part, of the vision of Theodor Herzl and his cadre of Zionist dreamers. It also marks the Palestinian Nakba. This convergence of the Jewish and Palestinian narratives is at the heart of the Israel-Palestine struggle itself, and of the struggle over the struggle in the two Diasporas.

After World War II, with the increasing clashes between Arab and Jewish militias, the British were looking for a way out of Palestine. This led directly to the UN partition plan, pushed for by the United States, injecting new energy into the Zionist cause. The plan was accepted by the Jews but rejected by the Palestinians and the Arab states supporting them.

The problem for Palestinians was twofold. First, the UN partition plan was seen as dividing up land that they saw as entirely their rightful territory. Second, if it was to be divided, the partition gave a great deal more land to the Jews than was reasonable based on the size of the two populations.[25]

Jews and Palestinians view the UN partition plan very differently. Most Jews see the plan as a credible, world-sanctioned resolution that made the founding of the State of Israel possible. For Palestinians, the world powers gave the Jews what was not theirs to give. The common refrain for supporters of Zionism is, "If only the Palestinians had accepted the UN plan, the horrors of the 1948 war and the consequences to Palestinians would never have occurred." In essence, it is the victim's fault for their victimization. Of course, Palestinians do not see this positively.

This failure of the UN partition plan led to war, fought in two phases, between late 1947 and early 1949. The first phase was a "civil war," fought between the Palestinian and Jewish populations, triggered by the rejection of the UN partition plan by the Arab Higher Committee for Palestine (AHCP). It was an armed resistance by

Palestinian militias against Jewish militias, attempting to prevent the takeover of their land. In the second phase, several Arab states joined the conflict, creating an "Arab-Israeli" war (or they invaded Israel, depending on your perspective) after Israel declared its independence. These Arab states had only recently gained their own independence, and their armies were woefully ill-equipped and poorly trained.

Israel signed separate armistice agreements with the individual Arab countries between January and July of 1949, formally ending the war. The consequences of the war for Arab Palestinians are hard to fully absorb and, in fact, continue to reverberate today. Along with the many dead, about 750,000 Palestinian Arabs became refugees in surrounding countries, and approximately 400 Arab villages and towns were destroyed. The Armistice line now gave Israel about 78 percent of the total land of historic Palestine.

It is hard to overestimate what the Nakba has meant to Palestinians. It was much more than losing their home, land, and homeland—it was being told they could never go back. It was living as eternal refugees in countries that did not always accept them and often were hostile towards them. It was a loss of identity as they attempted to assimilate into identities not their own. It was the bitterness of defeat that would be repeated upon them over and over again. It was the loss of livelihood and enduring life in camps and squalor, in poverty and destitute, shamed and looked down upon—and where in instances they would be bombed and massacred.

It was, and is still, a life of eternal relocation for many: to the West Bank or Gaza in 1948; from there to a neighboring Arab country in 1967; from a neighboring Arab country to a Western country when civil wars would erupt in those countries (such as in Lebanon or Syria). The parallels to the Jewish history of fleeing and relocating from various hostile diasporas in Europe are important to understand.

The 1948 war, and subsequent wars in 1967 and 1973,[26] contain multiple narratives: who attacked whom, what was "defensive" and what was "offensive," and ultimately, who is responsible. These are more than points for debate. Rather, they frame how each group relates to the struggle as a whole and how they view the Other.

Many Jews, including progressives, justify the 1948 war with responses such as, "They rejected the partition plan," "They attacked us," "There were massacres, but they happened to Jews as well," "Some were forced to leave, but many left on their own," and "War is war, and terrible things happen." While parsing these statements is not our prime concern here, what is important is that for every fallback defense, there is another side. The Arabs did reject the partition plan, but would Jews have accepted what the Arabs perceived as such a lopsided agreement if it were offered to them? The argument of "they attacked us" is more nuanced. In the first stage of the war, there were attacks and counterattacks by both Jewish and Palestinian militias. In the second phase of the war, the Arab states did "attack," but some saw this as a defensive measure to keep the Palestinian militias from being overrun.

The debate around the size and scope of the massacres, or the number of Palestinians who fled versus those expelled, is complicated. As we discussed in the introduction around the massacre at Deir Yassin, and while the numbers have been fiercely debated, the terror that such events engendered, which led directly to a vast number of refugees, cannot be overstated. Similarly, the perceived threat for Jews of the Arab resistance to Israel, especially in its close proximity to the Holocaust, must also be understood. For many Jews, "they rejected the partition plan" and "they attacked us" are much more than excuses. They are generally accepted rationales that explain that Jews did not set out to cause the harm inflicted on Palestinians, and had the Arab states acted differently, there would have been a different outcome.

Jews and Palestinians are two traumatized peoples, two victimized peoples, with two fractured identities. This fracturing has occurred as a result of long-term trauma, leaving both groups debilitated by the experiences of the past, causing them to turn inward and resist alternative narratives. We must come to terms with this if we are to begin to hear each other differently.

The debate about Zionism often centers around its intentions: Was it purely an establishment of a safe haven for Jews? Was the intention more benign than the actual result? Was there a purposeful attempt to clear out Palestinian Arabs in an act of ethnic cleansing? Did the Zionist leaders at the time of the founding of Israel intend to colonize the land?

This last point must be viewed through the eyes of late-nineteenth-century Europeans. Colonization, with all of its harmful outcomes, is separate from what we refer to today as "settler-colonialism," where the intent is to remove or at least diminish the native population and replace them with the "settler." Some believe that the early Zionists did not envision this particularly malevolent iteration of colonialism, rather expecting that there would be a level of coexistence with the existing population. Others, including Ze'ev Jabotinsky, an original Zionist, were clear that there was a native population that eventually would need to be resettled elsewhere. (For an in-depth look at Jabotinsky and his more ardent (than Herzl's) vision of Zionism, see *Jabotinsky: A Life* by Hillel Halkin.) While some are caught up in whether or not settler-colonialism is baked into the Zionist project, for our purposes here, we focus on the reality that the impact of Zionism on Palestinians mirrors most of the key features of settler-colonialism: displacement of the indigenous population, confiscation of property, and a state structure that is systemically discriminatory.

Solving these conflicting narratives is never our intent. What is essential is that in the discourse between the two Diasporas, we understand what Zionism means to each group. It is also important to focus more on the realities of Zionism for Palestinians than to excuse them with arguments of good intentions.

The push and pull over Israel in the West centers around Jewish self-determination versus Palestinian human rights and justice for all. The nuance needed in our two Diasporas is the need to separate justice for Palestinians from Jewish safety. These two necessities are seen as antithetical, or a zero-sum paradigm. Palestinian justice is seen as a risk to Jewish safety, and the parameters set to maintain Jewish safety ensure that justice for Palestinians is never realized.

A grieving Palestinian father, who works closely with a bereaved Jewish Israeli father (both lost a daughter to violence in Israel-Palestine) to foster peace and understanding, reflects on this idea:

"There cannot be security for Israelis without freedom for Palestinians, and there cannot be freedom for Palestinians without security for Israelis."[27] This co-reality is an essential paradox that needs to be seen as a shared need rather than a contested ideal.

Zionism, except for a very small part of the Jewish community known as the far Left, is a taken-for-granted necessity. To the majority of Jews, Zionism is a central, immovable part of Judaism. A Jewish-Israeli filmmaker, after immigrating to Canada, put it this way:

> "I think the whole Jewish nationalism, Zionism has taken over in North America, especially the way it has replaced the identity of being religious and an observant Jew. So I might get married with non-Jews, not eat kosher, etc. I am Jewish and I am Zionist and I support Israel, that is my identity."[28]

The debates in the Jewish Diaspora are not over the value of Zionism but rather over policy, governance, and how to end the conflict. Mission statements from even the most progressive Jewish organizations begin with a foundational statement about the right of Jewish self-determination and support for the State of Israel. Through the normalizing of the Zionist narrative in the Jewish Diaspora, the narrative of Palestinians has been pushed entirely to the sidelines.

As in the stories of the Three Little Pigs and Goldilocks, the wolf and the distressed damsel are the focus of our attention, not the pigs or the occupants of the little house in the woods. This is another way that the interplay between the mainstreamed muscularity and marginalized resistance narratives serve to frame the discourse in the two Diasporas.

It is essential to grasp that the Nakba is not limited to the events of 1947–1949. For Palestinians, the threat started with the first wave of Jewish immigration in the latter half of the nineteenth century, deepened after the Balfour Declaration, was cemented by the founding of Israel in 1948, continues each and every day, and shows no signs of abating. The daily grind of the Occupation, the expansion of the settlements, the arrests and killings of Palestinians, and the seeming impossibility of any serious recognition of their suffering causes Palestinians to relive the traumas of the Nakba on a daily basis.

ZIONISM AND THE NAKBA

"Suffering is the monopoly of no one."
—Edward Said, from the film *Knowledge Is the Beginning* (2005),
directed by Paul Smaczny

In order to begin a new conversation around Zionism and the Nakba, we need to grapple with the inseparable relationship between the two. The two metanarratives of the Holocaust and the Nakba, as we framed them in the introduction, are the internal engines of identity, trauma, and victimhood that resonate so deeply within each group.

As we have charted, Zionism began well before the Holocaust and the conflict between Jews and Palestinians in historic Palestine. However, the Holocaust, for Zionists, created a new urgency to form a Jewish state in Palestine.

In an interview, discussing their book *The Holocaust and the Nakba: A New Grammar of Trauma and History*, editors Bashir and Goldberg state that "the Nakba is a fundamental part of Israeli and Zionist history for which Israelis have to take responsibility, while the Holocaust is—in a very different way—also a part of Palestinian history because they could not avoid its local consequences and its global significance."[29]

The Holocaust, while not an ongoing oppression for Jews in the way the Nakba is for Palestinians, still holds a sense of "never-endingness," certainly at the psycho-traumatic level. *Apolis*, a 2017 film created for the peace-building group Telos, begins with the Jewish narrator saying, "In the West, virtually every Jew, in some way or another, is a Holocaust survivor."[30] It is impossible to overstate the shadow of the Holocaust; it permeates Jewish life, in Israel and in the Diaspora.

These two traumas, the Holocaust and the Nakba, are enmeshed together. Yet, in the public sphere, the Holocaust has dominated the narrative. The Holocaust is treated as inherently separate from all other genocides and world tragedies, and has, in the words of a character in *Apolis*, "become a collective human memory"; Jewish trauma is an exceptionalist narrative and holds a preeminent place in mainstream consciousness. We will look more deeply at how this has happened in Part III, but it is important to understand that, for many Jews, the time to hear testimony from those who lived through the Holocaust is nearing an end. As this generation will not be with us much longer, this fact brings with it great uncertainty of how and by whom the Holocaust will be remembered. Holocaust memory is a key part of the Jewish narrative, as is Nakba memory for Palestinians. We need to keep this in mind as we look at the discourse around Holocaust and Nakba memory in North America today.

In a review of *Apolis* that ran in the New York City-based Jewish newspaper *The Algemeiner*, writer Noah Summers excoriated both the film and the organization that inspired it, stating, "The template is all too familiar—those 'peace activists' who compare present-day Palestinian suffering to Jewish suffering during the Holocaust, simply as a ploy to engender sympathy for the Palestinian cause."[31] These types of rebuttals are very familiar, and they effectively tap into the Jewish trauma created by the long reach of the Holocaust. The message to Palestinians is that the act of making your story visible is a form of antisemitism that threatens Israel's security and even its existence.

We need to reframe how we teach the Holocaust and its connection to Zionism. In "Myths and Facts: Zionism and Reform Judaism," Rabbi Michael Marmur recounts how thousands of Israeli children travel to Poland every year, "wrapped in an Israeli flag, walk through the death camps and are expected to return home motivated to defend the motherland." He suggests, "we have to find another story to tell our children, one that does not root a philosophy of life in a collective memory of death.[32] Marmur is pushing all of us to challenge the understanding of trauma as a tribal experience, which, by necessity, excludes the trauma of another. Antisemitism is the trauma that mandates the defense of Zionism, viewing Zionism as both a curative and preventive response to not just the Holocaust but to antisemitism in its totality.

The Palestinian-American intellectual Edward Said also called on Palestinians to engage with the Jewish Holocaust experience. The documentary we quote from at the beginning of this section, *Knowledge Is the Beginning*, charts the amazing musical project spearheaded by Said and Israeli conductor Daniel Barenboim that brings together young Palestinian and Jewish musicians to form the West-Eastern Divan Orchestra. During a visit to Germany, the young musicians go on a tour of the Buchenwald concentration camp. Said is seen encouraging the Arab musicians to go on the tour and deeply engage in what they see.

What is so essential that Said is revealing here is that to engage with the Other—and the trauma of the Other—is not an equivocation or a diminishing of your own experience. Said was an extremely important and influential advocate for Palestinian rights and sovereignty, for which many pro-Israel groups have continuously excoriated him. We can and must do both: engage with the Other's trauma and resist oppression and inequality.

Like antisemitism, Zionism resonates entirely differently for Jews than it does for Palestinians. In fact, sustaining the Zionist narrative requires diminishing, or even dismissing, the consequences of Zionism to Palestinians. This begins with the need to diminish the events of 1948, the Nakba. There are many extreme examples, such as the 2011 "Nakba Law" that allowed the Israeli minister of finance to deny funding to any institution that commemorates the Nakba. Also, through yearly counterdemonstrations at Nakba remembrance events and its infamous booklet "Nakba-Nonsense," the group Im Tzura peddles the notion that the Nakba is a myth propagated by Palestinians to deflect blame for their attempt to wipe out Jews in the 1948 war.

This works to lessen the scope and depth of the conversation about the Nakba. Due partly to the dominance of the Holocaust narrative, many Palestinians are reluctant to fully absorb the depth of the trauma of the Holocaust for Jews. Both groups must deal with each other's trauma, as it is at the root of every facet of the conflict. Currently, neither group, in its mainstream, is doing this.

While these types of propaganda can be peddled by both sides, it is important to understand the force of the deeply ingrained resistance in the discourse around the conflict to acknowledging the depth of Palestinian suffering. Zionism is imbued with an unresolvable conundrum: the liberation and security of the Jewish people, created by the establishment of the State of Israel, caused the dislocation, dispossession, and oppression of Palestinians.

This is not something that simply happened; it is still happening.

This conundrum presents Diaspora Jews with several challenges. First, if they accept this, what does that say about the moral and ethical standing of Jews in the world today? Israeli lawyer and Palestinian rights activist Daniel Seidemann framed the progressive Jewish conundrum this way: "Are they fighting to defend Palestinians or are they fighting to get an Israel they can live with?"[33] These types of questions can cause a fissure between one's Jewish identity and one's ethical compass. In other words, is progressive Zionism about protecting Israel while minimizing guilt, or is it a true movement for justice for Palestinians, even if that endangers a Jewish majority state in Israel?

One of the perils of social justice work is assuming that one oppressed group has de facto sympathy for another oppressed group. The inability to see another's suffering, particularly when it is entwined with your own in some way, is particularly difficult. While it is relatively easy, cognitively, to recognize that Palestinians were not responsible for the Holocaust or the centuries of Jewish oppression in Europe, in Palestine-Jewish dialogue, this does not always seem clear. Discourse, steeped in trauma and centuries of victimization, creates an illogical sense of victimhood and who is to blame for this victimization.

Since Israel is seen, both symbolically and literally, as the escape from oppression, even from another Holocaust, the defense of Israel becomes an existential necessity. This defense tacitly discourages grasping the cost, to Palestinians, of Israel's formation and ongoing existence. This phenomenon is similar to what occurs in the discourse on antisemitism that we describe in the previous section.

For example, the IHRA definition of antisemitism, with most examples tied directly to Israel, is not an accident but a necessity. The more the debate is framed around protecting Jews from the sting of antisemitism, the less Palestinian rights and freedoms are considered. Similarly, the more Zionism is framed as liberation from an existential threat, the cost of this liberation to Palestinians can be diminished or dismissed.

The discourse around Zionism and antisemitism also aligns in that both are framed in terms of denying something to Jews. Antisemitism is seen as denying Jews the right to equal status under the law and safety from oppression, and resistance to Zionism is seen as denying Jews the right to self-determination.

The Centre for Israel and Jewish Affairs (CIJA), in a video entitled "Canadian Jewish Views: Episode 6," defended the IHRA definition of antisemitism, stating, "The vast majority of Canadian Jews are Zionists—then if you are anti-Zionist, you are anti the vast majority of Canadian Jews, and there is a word for that—antisemitism." This type of connection must be examined rather than dismissed. The statement suggests that challenging a group's political views is, in and of itself, a form of personal hatred of that group. Being an anti-Zionist is framed as being anti-Jewish rather than against its outcome: to resist the oppressive violation of human and political rights and property that Zionism inflicts on Palestinians. Jews feel, quite understandably, that they have been victimized, and they fear this victimization will continue to reoccur. However, the types of statements in the CIJA video operationalize victimhood rather than victimization. They politicize and weaponize victimhood. They falsely link criticism of Israel to hatred of Jews for the singular purpose of silencing criticism.

In the summer of 2020, a food store owner in Toronto posted on social media that the store was open only to non-racists and included the hashtag "Zionists not welcome," creating an intense debate that is typical of the wall we are pointing to.

CIJA led the response from the Canadian-Jewish community, citing it as hate speech and blatantly racist, comparing the post to signs from the 1940s that read "No Jews or dogs allowed." Similar to the video referenced earlier, much of the commentary linked criticism of Zionism to hating Jews. The logic being "as the vast majority of Canadian Jews are Zionists, so if Zionists are not welcome, then Jews are not welcome." Social media was filled with responses (and responses to the responses) producing little if any meaningful discourse. Instead, there was the usual tribal screaming and insults directed at those with opposing views, on both sides of the argument.

In much of the back-and-forth, blanket statements about Zionism are hurled. One post states "Zionism is a colonial enterprise" and another fires back "Zionism is an anti-colonial enterprise, resisting the Arab colonialists, creating freedom for an oppressed people." Viewing the store owner's post from the lens of antisemitism is a very effective way to silence debate and avoid a nuanced reading of the post. Is it reasonable to conclude that "Zionists are not welcome" means barring all Jews, or is it more likely that this was a political statement, however crudely put, resisting the consequences of Zionism to Palestinians? In fact, there is an embossed decal in the store window, stating "I Love Gaza," not "I Hate Jews."

Imagine a response to the owner that seeks healing rather than division and zero-sum victories:

"I am a Jew and I felt quite hurt by your social media post, particularly the hashtag 'Zionists not welcome.' What do you mean by Zionists? Do you mean all people who have an affinity for Israel? Do you distinguish people who have no interest in what is happening to Palestinians from those, like me, who value Israel but have deep concerns over what Israel has become, particularly its harmful effects on Palestinians? Would you please clarify what you meant, and be clearer in the future so that we can all learn and listen to each other with an ear towards healing, rather than further division?"

If one were to respond in this manner, it might be possible to learn rather than demonize. The sad reality is that CIJA and groups like it are more interested in deepening the divide in the discourse about Israel-Palestine and the struggle, reinforcing an us vs. them paradigm. By responding to a hurtful post with such force (calling for a boycott of the store, pressuring its business partners to discontinue their relationship with it and even vandalizing the store window) the hurt is only magnified. We can be hurt and still listen. Another can offend us without us dismissing them.

The possibilities created by thinking outside of an identity, trauma, and victimhood narrative create access to an escape route from zero-sum discourses. Recognizing that the owner of the post and those who read it both have legitimacy, that both are in need of being heard and having their views respected—all of this is necessary to begin to dismantle the wall between.

"Zionists not welcome" was taken to mean "Those who see Israel as the hope and realization of a Jewish homeland are not welcome," rather than, "What is not welcome is the injustice suffered by Palestinians that this realization has caused." Both matter. We need to understand more fully what Zionism means to a Jew and to a Palestinian.

For a Jew, Zionism and historic Jewish suffering are intrinsically linked and go to the heart of the Jewish experience and identity. What the land of historic Palestine is—known biblically as the Land of Israel or *Eretz Yisrael* has cultural, religious, and spiritual meaning for most Jews. If one went to Hebrew school or had even a minimal Jewish education through a synagogue, the stories from the Torah and the haftarah (a collection of books from the prophets) are not just located in the land but are related to the land. The stories are "in place," they exist as part of Jericho, Judea, Samaria, Mount Sinai, and Canaan ("the promised land"). While it is reasonable to view the biblical connection to the land as separate from legally binding own-ership of the land, dismissing its importance is counterproductive. It is significant that in every synagogue, the Ark (which contains the Torah scrolls) faces east, towards Jerusalem. Even "cultural Jews" have at least some affinities for many of these stories and traditions.

The Jewish history of displacement is juxtaposed with "having a land." The stories of the *Tanakh* (Hebrew Bible) are stories of re-peated oppression, and loss of religious and cultural "place," including the destruction of the First and Second temples. Perhaps the most well-known story in the Torah is the oppression of the Jewish people as slaves at the hand of the Pharaoh in Egypt, and Moses leading them out of slavery and into the promised land. This story is retold every year in most Jewish homes, even those that are not particularly religious. The telling of the story in the Haggadah ends with the powerful words *L'Shana Haba'ah B'Yerushalayim* ("Next year in Jerusalem"), where Jews imagine having the Passover seder meal in Jerusalem the following year. This is the beckoning to Zion, the call home that resonates, at some level, for most Jews.

This story also creates a seemingly irresolvable tension; Jews are taught that the experience of slavery and the gift of freedom demand that Jews fight for freedom for everyone. It is traditional for the first-born Jewish male to fast the day of the first Passover meal (up until the seder), not for the purposes of remembering Jewish suffering but to mourn for the Egyptian first-born sons who were killed.[34] The spirit of empathy and understanding for the Other is at the root of Jewish teaching. In the final section of the book, we will explore how we might utilize such spiritual and religious values in creating a new discourse with and about the Other.

After the destruction of the second temple and the sacking of Jerusalem at the hands of the Romans in 70 CE, the Jews became, primarily, a diaspora people. Some remained though, and there has always been a Jewish presence in the land. While this point is debated in discourses surrounding who has legitimacy in the land, what is more significant may be that the biblical land of Israel was lost. While various invaders had previously displaced Jews, including the Babylonians and the Assyrians, the destruction of the Second Temple and of Jerusalem was a fatal blow from which the Jews did not begin to recover until the establishment of the State of Israel in 1948.

A major thrust of the Jewish-Palestinian discourse in the West is the question of who has legitimacy in the land. The concept of legitimacy is complicated. Jewish connection to the land is inarguable. Historic Palestine was the land of the Jews. How do we acknowledge this and still have frank conversations on how this history does not excuse or explain the cost that Zionism has exacted from Palestinians? Ideological debate around the historical significance of the land for Jews rests in "We were there, we have a right to it, you can't say that we don't have a right to it, we have been there for over 3,000 years." Conversely, it is too simple for Palestinians and their supporters to argue that the Jews have no right or historical connection to a land they used to live on more than 2,000 years ago. Both peoples have an historic claim to the land, but this must be nuanced. We do need to distinguish biblical and spiritual connection from the claim of a people that were the majority in the land since the Islamic conquest of Jerusalem in the twelfth century. But to ignore the Jewish claim entirely is also not reasonable.

In conversations between Jews and Palestinians (and their supporters) in the Diaspora, we need to hold multiple truths while seeking the most just outcome. Dismissing each other's claim to the land through narrow tropes of "Jews are not settlers, as we have always been there" or "Go back to Europe, this is not your land" does not lead to real learning and understanding.

The propaganda wars, however, are based on bolstering the claim of one side, often by trying to debunk the claim of the other. One of the central tenets of the pro-Israel lobby is that Israel is the lone democracy in the middle of a sea of authoritarian states. This reminder of Israel's stature as a democratic state is often utilized in order to deflect criticism of Israel and create an affinity with it for Western democracies. For Palestinians, this is problematic on several levels, but it gives many Jews a degree of comfort.

The "democracy" argument requires some deeper analysis, particularly from a perspective of the discourse between the two Diasporas. Much of the pro-Israel position is centered on seeing Israel as a victim. This victimhood taps into Jewish trauma in a very effective manner. It starts with the forming of the State of Israel and the events of 1948 and its close proximity to the Holocaust. A common sentiment goes something like, "Only three years from the Holocaust, when our democracy had just been formed, they attacked and tried to wipe us out."

In a 2019 video entitled "Why Don't You Support Israel?" former Canadian prime minister Stephen Harper defends Israel by arguing that Israel is the lone democracy in the Middle East.[35] This is appealing to Western sensibilities, creating the contrast between "us" (Judeo-Christian, democratic-loving countries) and "them" (Islamic, theocratic, authoritarian countries). The video portrays Israel as a peace-loving little country in the middle of a mass of Arab countries that are a constant threat, reminding the viewer that Israel's only crime is defending its democracy.

Israel and Zionism are, with little exception, shielded from criticism and wrapped in the protective arms of "fellow democracies." The Harper video, with its embedded racial undertones and demonizing of Arabs as terrorists, particularly Arab Muslims, brushes past the reality that Israel today is more accurately an "ethnocracy" than a democracy. However, our focus is how painting Israel as a victim serves to dismiss, again, the stories and experiences of Palestinians. Harper's question, "Why wouldn't I support Israel?" is framed entirely from the point of view that Israel is unfairly singled out for criticism. This, again, inflames victimhood and limits nuanced discourse on what the critique is actually about: the oppression of Palestinians.

Of course, a significant amount of pro-Palestinian views are promoted online, but they are rarely, if ever, touted by presidents, prime ministers, and other top officials from leading Western democracies. Instead, there is a tidal wave of state-supported bills, statements, and policies (like the adoption of the IHRA definition of antisemitism) that serve to support Israel and Zionism while minimizing and marginalizing the traumas and realities of Palestinians.

Perhaps the greatest challenge in building understanding between Jews and Palestinians in the West is that they are beginning from two entirely different places. Many progressive Jewish groups in the United States and Canada share a similar vision: "pro-Israel and pro-peace." They rest their hope of a lasting peace on a "two-state solution" based on the pre-1967 borders. The disconnect, though, is that their Palestinian partners in dialogue view the conflict through 1948 and the Nakba, not 1967. Yes, the Occupation, settlements, the security fence, checkpoints, military interventions, and loss of any basic human rights are an ongoing tragedy for Palestinians, but the wound, the trauma, is 1948. It is as if progressive Jews are yelling, "'67, '67, '67" and Palestinians are shouting back "'48, '48, '48"—and no one is hearing the other side.

We must create a space to speak honestly about '48 without being drawn into the black hole that conflates questioning Zionism with a disregard for Jewish safety and self-determination. We must be able to talk about 1948 if we are going to do meaningful work together.

Both the Holocaust, the trauma that propelled Israel's existence and maintains its necessity for Jews, and the resulting trauma of the Nakba for Palestinians, forms the "foundations" of the wall between. Israel, for Jews, is the fulfillment of the Zionist dream; it is a story of rising from the ashes of Auschwitz, a story of liberation, a partial righting of historical wrongs. It is the antithesis of all of this for Palestinians. While it represents Jewish liberation, for Palestinians it remains a settler-colonial project. While Israel is seen in the West as both a symbol and a concrete representation of Jewish freedom, some now see Israel as a settler-colonial enterprise, due to fifty-plus years of occupation, the expansion of settlements, and frequent threats of annexation. These two poles—of the intentions of Zionism and what Zionism has become—must both be taken seriously. From a trauma perspective, the need to sustain Israel, the relief from trauma, is the cause of another's trauma.

The debate must never be about who was more victimized by their respective histories, as both groups have experienced victimization, and still do. While Jews have experienced centuries of oppression at the hands of the powerful, Zionism, particularly from 1948 forward, gave Jews the power over another, weaker, opponent: the Palestinians. With a combination of military might, technical and social ingenuity, and the support of Western countries, especially the United States, Israel became a thriving nation-state and a formidable foe to anyone who would threaten it.

Zionism began primarily as a dream of Jewish self-determination, of a Jewish homeland. Israeli historian, Dimitry Shumsky states, "Before the 1940's, the aspiration for a nation-state was not central in the Zionist movement." However, as Peter Beinart points out, "The holocaust fundamentally transformed Jewish thinking," shifting Zionism from its original goal of creating a Jewish homeland to a demand for Jewish sovereignty.[36]

The victories of the wolf and the damsel came at the expense of the pigs and the residents of the little house. Zionism and the Nakba are entwined in each other. As Jews, quite reasonably, view Jewish trauma through the Holocaust, they must also understand that Palestinians see their trauma through the Nakba. Palestinians will never heal from a solely post-'67 solution. This is why recognition and regret of what happened in 1948 to Palestinians is an essential part of any lasting move forward. It is also impossible to overstate the necessity of a Jewish state for most Jews. It is not a convenience or a nicety; it is the one and only insurance policy against another Holocaust.

Today, Jews and Palestinians are irrevocably enmeshed in the two metanarratives of the Holocaust and the Nakba. As long as the recalling of one is used to silence the other, no real progress can be made.

CHAPTER 6
PALESTINIAN RESISTANCE

"Resistance is futile."
—The Borg, *Star Trek: The Next Generation*

Palestinians know their resistance is never welcome, no matter what shape it takes, whether it is in the form of art, literature, boycott, film, UN resolution, stones, or bullets. Since the dawn of the Zionist project, Palestinians have been resisting loss after further loss. *Muqawama* (Arabic for resistance) and *sumood* (resilience) have become part of the Palestinian ethos: resistance to oppression, injustice, occupation, dispossession, marginalization, victimization, demonization—and to the loss of identity.

Perhaps their proudest achievement is that they continue to resist (and therefore to exist). They tell their story, pass it on to the next generation, overcome squalid conditions, survive violence, and maintain faith in the justness of their cause. They resist the acceptance of defeat and remain an obstacle to the Zionist project; "a bone in the throat."

One Hebron family we know embodies the concept of *muqawama* in the names given to its children: Nedal ("struggle"), Jehad ("holy struggle"), Kefah ("fight"), Thaer ("rebel"), Fidaa ("self-sacrifice"), and Ammar (in reference to Yasser Arafat's nom de guerre, Abu Ammar).

In talking about Palestinians, David Ben-Gurion, Israel's first prime minister, is often quoted as having said, "The old will die and the young will forget." But to Palestinians, Palestine is not just a land lost. It is part of the soul, integral to the self, central to a Palestinian's identity. It is a legend that transcends generations. Palestine is larger-than-life and an ideal worth living and dying for. The land was lost, but the idea of Palestine remains central. The old did die, but the young did not forget.

To Jews, Palestinian resistance is an existential threat, not only to Israel but also to Jews as a people. Their trauma, induced by a history of displacement and oppression, culminating in the Holocaust, and accompanied by repeated acts of antisemitism today, has them relating to Israel as both a temporal state and a solution to historic oppression. It signifies the preservation of self because Israel symbolizes an oasis where Jews do not get murdered. A threat to Israel is therefore a threat to self. And Israel faces an *existential threat on a daily basis.* Hence, Jewish resistance to Palestinian resistance develops from a place of historic trauma, a feeling of dread that overwhelms them in a manner that may often be greater than any actual threat. Whether or not the threat is realistic, it feels real and therefore it is.

Palestinians view Israel as an omnipotent military force that has defeated them and the combined Arab armies at every turn. They see it as an army that exercises control over Palestinian life to the point of suffocation. They see it as a force that is endlessly supported and made stronger by Western governments. They see its ultra-powerful lobbies that dictate Middle East policy to Western governments. Israel is Goliath.

Jews, on the other hand, see Israel as a small country surrounded by hostile forces that never cease trying to destroy it. They see it standing against fifty-seven Islamic states that don't miss a chance to discredit it at the UN. They wonder why the 1.8 billion Muslims of the world won't allow its 14 million Jews to have this small sliver of land called Israel to call their own. Israel is David.

To Jews, Palestinian resistance means terrorism and the destruction of Israel. It means Islamist fanatics willing to blow themselves up to kill Jews—and destroy Israel. It means Hamas hurling rockets at Sderot to kill innocent Jews—and destroy Israel. It means boycotts that aim to discredit Israel *in order to destroy it*. It means accusations of apartheid aimed at smearing Israel *in order to destroy it*. It means Islamic countries ganging up to demonize Israel in international forums *in order to destroy it*.

To Palestinians, resistance is a philosophical and existential condition. As long as they resist, their will cannot be broken. As long as they resist, they will continue to exist. As long as they resist, they remain the bane of the Zionist project. They resist by any means: "over there" (in Israel-Palestine), through defiance, martyrdom, and jihad, and over here (in the North American diaspora), through advocacy, boycotts, art, film, poetry, music, and theater.

PALESTINIAN RESISTANCE – OVER THERE

As you read, it is essential to keep in mind that the Israeli narrative of overcoming seemingly insurmountable odds over a hostile Arab majority in the region has likely influenced how you view Palestinian resistance. While some in the region would argue that the 1967 and 1973 wars were about redressing the losses of 1948, this doesn't diminish the traumatic memory of Jews who lived through them. In 1967, Israel engaged in a preemptive strike against Egypt, Syria, and Jordan, whose armies were amassed on its borders, following a period of rhetorical threats by Arab leaders of "driving the Jews to the sea." In 1973, Egypt and Syria were a real threat to the Jewish state until the United States intervened with an "air bridge" of military supplies and equipment.

But these threats do not exist today. While an Arab-Israeli conflict did in fact exist between Israel and the Arab countries bordering it (Egypt, Jordan, Syria, Lebanon) for decades, the peace pacts between Israel and Egypt (1979) and between it and Jordan (1994) effectively ended the unified Arab stand against Israel. In 2020, as part of what was called the Abraham Accords, five Arab countries (United Arab Emirates, Bahrain, Morocco, Oman, and Sudan) normalized relations with Israel.

Today, the only remaining threats to Israel come from Iran (not an Arab state) and its allies in Lebanon and Syria (both being nearly failed states). To those who view the regional conflict as one between Western interests represented by the US-Israel axis versus Arab nationalist/Palestinian interests, the only ones left on the latter side are the Palestinians themselves. And while the current Iranian regime and its Lebanese and Syrian allies do maintain an anti-Israel stance, it is to serve the regional interests of the Iranian regime and its allies and not necessarily those of the Palestinians.

The skewed view of the struggle (Israel versus everyone else) has allowed us to forget that the Occupation is, by definition and practice, violent. As an example, any Palestinian, anywhere in the West Bank, can be removed from their home by Israeli soldiers, in the middle of the night, on any day, for any reason. They can then be held for prolonged periods (called administrative detention) without any charges.[37] Thousands of children have been reportedly arrested in such night raids and subjected to abuses.[38] Palestinians have been living under a repressive military rule since 1967.

They have no basic rights.

Some other illustrations of Palestinian life under occupation:

- Palestinians have to start their day very early in the morning to go to work because of the hours they will have to spend at Israeli checkpoints placed outside and in-between Palestinian cities and towns.
- They are rarely given permits to build or expand their homes, and if they decide to build anyway, their new structures are demolished by Israeli army bulldozers.
- Armed Israeli settlers often harass or attack Palestinian homes and olive groves with near-total impunity.
- The separation wall has kept Palestinian communities from each other, from East Jerusalem (with its religious and cultural landmarks), and in some cases from the land they cultivate
- Palestinian demonstrators, including children, are often shot and killed without repercussions.

- Palestinian land can be abruptly confiscated for a variety of reasons: building new Jews-only settlements, building new Jews-only access roads to these settlements, and any variety of security explanations.

This is only a partial list of the daily humiliations and oppressions an average West Bank Palestinian can face. For Palestinians in Gaza, it is a much worse situation. While Israel no longer technically occupies Gaza, it has full control over its daily life: its borders, airspace, and territorial waters. Gaza has been under a complete Israeli blockade since 2007, with cooperation by Egypt on its own border with Gaza. Entering or leaving Gaza is restricted to most and requires a special permit. All goods, including electricity, fuel, water, medicine, building materials, etc., that enter or leave the territory are under Israeli control.

Gaza is one of the most densely populated places on the planet (approximately 2 million people live in a 365-kilometer area), where people live in extreme poverty and unemployment hovers around 50 percent. Most Gazans don't get to leave the strip—ever. It's been accurately described as "the world's largest open-air prison."

The people of Gaza live a violent existence. Yet, to us on the outside, it is largely invisible. We in the West see Palestinians similarly to how we saw "red Indians" in mid-twentieth-century Hollywood westerns: attacking caravans of innocent white people for no apparent reason except that they're violent savages. When Palestinians resist their oppression with violence of their own, it looks to us as if it has come out of nowhere. We see images of teenagers throwing rocks at Israeli army vehicles, of suicide bombers blowing up a civilian bus, of Hamas launching crude rockets into southern Israel, and of men and women marching in anger, shouting "*Allahu akbar!*" (Arabic for "God is great!"). When we see groups of men wearing kaffiyehs (the checkered Palestinian headdresses often associated with resistance) carrying coffins, brandishing weapons, and waving flags. When we see hordes of people, men, women, young and old, marching towards the Israeli border with Gaza, slinging stones at the soldiers amid tear gas and flying bullets in the March of Return (2019), our association of Arabs with terrorism is confirmed. We seem unable to distinguish these images from the suicide bombers and Hamas rockets; they all get lumped together in our minds as violent acts against a benign force.

From our view in the West, we see nothing elegant. What we see appears chaotic and flailing at best, and unhinged, backward, violent, and terroristic at worst. We don't witness the daily violence of Palestinian lives. We forget their ongoing oppression and humiliation. So, when Israel claims it is only trying to keep order and defend itself from violence, we believe it. It *is* believable, because that's mostly the only side we hear. The violent lives of Palestinians are only visible to us when they themselves inflict violence on Jews.

But...

To Palestinians, all of these barbaric-seeming activities are acts of *muqawama*, resistance to the conditions in which they live: total military rule, house demolitions, restrictions on movement, humiliation at checkpoints, inability to eke a living, and decades of subjugation. It is resistance so that Palestine, the idea and the ideal, can continue. It is resistance to slow Zionism down. For Zionism, literally, is killing them.

No, it isn't elegant. It is messy, frustrated, and disempowered. And when Israeli civilians in buses and cafes are targeted in acts of terror, the situation is turned on Palestinians. Their legitimate struggle for freedom and self-determination becomes reduced, sometimes intentionally, to acts of terrorism. This silences their voices and allows others to take away any remaining agency. It allows those responsible for their oppression to claim that it is legitimate. It allows those seeking to make peace with them doubt their motives and shy away from them.

But...

What do we know about what one is prepared to do after more than fifty-five years of occupation and oppression? Or after more than a decade of a suffocating, crippling blockade? Do you resist with what you have (crude rockets that can't be guided to proper targets)? Do you try to inflict pain, so the pain inflicted on you does not go unanswered? Do you resist, for the sake of *muqawama*, so your cause remains alive and your hopes are not crushed? Do you maintain the resistance as a way to remain alive—although the resistance itself might get you killed?

You do something often enough and a certain label sticks to you. Palestinian militants have resorted to terrorist acts too many times in the past decades, which, not only inflicted great harm on civilians, but also harmed the cause of Palestinian struggle for freedom. In the 1970s, they hijacked planes and attacked the Munich Olympics where they killed Israeli athletes as the world watched.

And while the First Intifada brought the world's attention and sympathy to Palestinians resisting the occupation, the Second Intifada saw suicide attacks on cafes and civilian busses inside Israel intensify greatly. These attacks created a justification for building the separation wall and led to the marginalization of the Israeli peace movement.

Better leadership should prevail. Clearer strategies are needed. Creative solutions have to come forward.

But...

How do you resist F-16s when you have none? How do you resist the best in military technology when all you have are home-made explosives? How do you resist a long history of loss when your future looks just as bleak? How do you resist an army that has the full backing of the United States? To Palestinians, the answer is through martyrdom and jihad. In the words of a desperate character in the Netflix series *Ozark,* "If you know you have a future, there's no reason to blow up anything in the present."

For us in the West, jihad is a dirty word. We forget the muja-hideen we celebrated and supported against the Soviet invasion of Afghanistan in the 1980s. "Freedom fighters," we called them. They were Islamist. Very. And we didn't mind. We forget that a *mujahid* is someone who exercises jihad: holy struggle. After the Soviets abandoned Afghanistan and jihad stopped being ours, we started referring to the meaning of the word as "holy war," instead of "holy struggle." So, when Palestinian Islamic jihad attacks (resists?) Israel with crude missiles, they are seen as terrorists, not freedom fighters.

The same goes for martyrdom. Contrary to popular belief, the concept of martyrdom is not central to Islam, nor is the idea of killing oneself in the fight against an enemy. We've seen martyrdom by Japanese kamikaze fighter pilots in the Second World War, and suicide attacks were a popular tactic of the Liberation Tigers of Tamil Eelam in Sri Lanka.

In Islam, the Arabic meaning of the word "martyr," *shaheed*, is someone who gives his life for the sake of a cause or a belief system. During the heyday of Islamic conquests, martyrdom was closely associated with battle, and, while fighting, one gained "one of the two best outcomes" (Quran 9:52): victory or martyrdom. Therefore, martyrdom was second only to victory, and was in itself part of a victorious process.

The concept of dying for one's country was also present in pre-state Israel: *Tov Lamut Be'ad Artzeinu*. "The choice to fight and die rather than flee became the bedrock of a military and political doctrine of bravery ... [and] the mantra of Zionist heroism."[39]

To Palestinians, martyrdom has come to symbolize resistance and resilience, which, as we explained, are essential to their continued existence. Every Palestinian who is killed while resisting the Occupation is given the honorific title of *shaheed*. Even people who die of natural causes are often given that title because, well, they died while living—surviving, persisting—under the Occupation.

To Jews and many in the West, Palestinian martyrdom is associated with violence and terrorism, as the act of fanatics—worse, barbarians—who do not value human life and are willing to squander it, in a gross and grisly manner. It is seen as a cult of death.

In the West, we do not associate Palestinian resistance with a simple act of defiance by a sixteen-year-old, fair-skinned blond girl. The story of Ahed Tamimi made headlines in 2017, when she pushed, slapped, and kicked an Israeli soldier, and a video of the incident, shot by her cousin in front of her home in the West Bank village of Nabi Saleh, went viral. The Tamimi family had a history of "organizing weekly protests against the expansion of a nearby Israeli settlement, gatherings that sometimes turned to stone-throwing, prompting Israeli troops to respond with tear gas, rubber bullets, and sometimes live fire."[40.] On the day in question, Ahed claims Israeli soldiers had shot her cousin in the face with a rubber bullet, angering her and her mother into confronting them.

"Palestinians celebrated Ahed as a hero. Cartoons, posters and murals portrayed her as a Joan of Arc-like character, confronting the Israeli military with her mane of long, dirty-blond curls flowing in the breeze,"[41] wrote the Associated Press. To Israelis, Ahed and her family are nothing but troublemakers, out to delegitimize Israel by presenting themselves as David in a fight against Goliath.

Within days of the incident, the Israeli military, in an overnight raid, entered the Tamimis' house and arrested Ahed and her mother. They were sentenced to eight months in prison. Some in the Israeli media accused Ahed of not being a Palestinian because of her European features, and only acting like one to make Israel look bad. Michael Oren, Israel's deputy minister for public diplomacy and a former ambassador to the United States, acknowledged leading a secret investigation into whether the Tamimis were "real" Palestinians.

At first, many in the Israeli public were proud of the restraint shown by the soldiers, but soon they began to see the Tamimi incident as a threat to the image of the decisiveness portrayed by the Israeli army. A prominent and influential Israeli journalist, Ben Kaspit, wrote in an op-ed that "a price could be better exacted from Tamimi on another occasion, in the dark, without witnesses and cameras."[42]

After finishing her sentence, Ahed went on a victory tour in the Middle East and Europe. She was hailed as a hero and honored by presidents of countries and other public figures for symbolizing the endurance of the Palestinian resistance. In Spain, she met fabled footballer Butragueno of the soccer team Real Madrid and received a team jersey with her name on it. This prompted Israel's foreign ministry spokesman, Emmanuel Nahshon, to call the team's embrace of Tamimi "shameful" in a Twitter post. "It would be morally wrong to stay silent while a person inciting hatred and violence goes on a victory tour as if she is some kind of rock star," he wrote.[43]

That such a courageous yet simple act would elicit such strong and opposite reactions from Israelis and Palestinians speaks volumes about the significance and symbolism of Palestinian resistance to both sides. While it's understandable that Palestinians would celebrate Ahed, the threat of this celebration to Israel highlights the vulnerability felt by many Jews.

The Tamimi incident is indicative of the depth of the relationship between Israel, including the image it projects to the world, and the survival of the Jewish people. Logically, Ahed did not pose a real threat to the soldier, much less to the State of Israel. But she posed a threat to how Israel is viewed, and therefore how Jews are viewed. For the Zionist narrative to work, Jews must be the victims of aggressive Arab Palestinians and must always appear victorious. When this narrative was challenged, the pro-Israel lobby pulled all the stops to counter how Israel was being perceived.

Our ongoing goal in this book is to create spaces where we can reflect, distinguish past trauma from present threats, and reimagine the Other as they exist in their world, not how we might imagine them in ours.

PALESTINIAN RESISTANCE – OVER HERE

The political roots of how the pro-Israel narrative has so overwhelmed the Palestinian narrative rests largely in the important place Israel has maintained in Western democracies, especially the United States. Israel would not have survived as an entity for too long had it not been for the financial, moral, political, and military support of Western democracies, primarily from the United States.

Three primary factors are behind this support: "strategic interests in the Middle East, the perception of shared values, and the political engagement of Jews and their allies," writes Zack Beauchamp, a senior correspondent at Vox.[44] While strategic interests can shift and little can be done to control them, the latter two factors are where pro-Israel lobbies focus their efforts in order to maintain cohesive Western support of Israel in the Diaspora.

The perception of shared values is dependent on Israel being seen by the public as very much "like us," that is, a Western-style democracy with the political freedoms, rule of law, and a rights-based society that comes with it. Israel has successfully branded itself as "the only democracy in the Middle East," distinguishing itself from the sea of authoritarian regimes (the Arab countries) that surround it. Despite that claim not being accurate (Lebanon, Turkey, and more recently Tunisia are also democracies—imperfect and struggling as they are), it stuck by being repeated so often by so many people in power.

As for political engagement, Beauchamp states that Jews and their Christian Evangelical allies "are two of the most politically engaged groups in the United States." He also describes the pro-Israel lobby as one of the strongest political lobbies in the country. Among other factors, this contributes to "congressional votes on issues relating to Israel [being] famously lopsided," and "many pro-Israel bills and resolutions [passing] unanimously in the Senate."

Sophisticated, well-funded, and highly effective Jewish organizations have not only ensured that a powerful pro-Israel voice speaks loudly and clearly, they have also mobilized a community that is both civically and politically active, and highly committed to Israel and Zionism. These organizations have worked hard to ensure that resistance to Palestinian resistance over here is at least as strong as it is over there.

Those who are satisfied with the status quo (Israel being militarily dominant and maintaining the support of the West) are loath to see any resistance to it. The sense of "security" provided by the status quo, in response to historic trauma, creates the perception that any form of resistance to it is violent and potentially life-threatening.

Those who are unhappy with the status quo because of the violence it inflicts on daily Palestinian life are loath to see it supported. Their own trauma drives them to perceive those who are in favor of it as complicit with, and actual enablers of, the perpetrators of violence and are therefore prepared to do everything in their power to resist them.

In sum, to one side, resistance to the status quo is violent. To the other, the status quo is itself violent, eliciting resistance to it. One resistance begets the other, and we end up with a cycle of resistance.

There is little physical violence here in the Diaspora, but there are constant confrontations—in the media, on university campuses, and in discourses. Confrontations between two ill-matched adversaries: elegant institutions on one side, flailing (by comparison) groups on the other.

The Jewish communities in North America are older and much better established and organized than their Palestinian counterparts. Their institutions are well-financed, staffed and professionally run by North American-born individuals; Palestinian ones tend to be run mostly by volunteers, many of them foreign-born and speak with an accent (something that has started changing in the recent decade). Pro-Israel organizations consistently synchronize with the government of Israel on messaging and combine to create an elaborate machinery of media and government relations. The PLO doesn't even have a media office in DC.

The short of it is that Palestinians are not only mismatched by their enemies over there, but by their adversaries over here. They are the David to Goliath again. Anyone with doubts about this need only look at the voting record in support of Israel in both US houses of Congress, where politicians compete to outdo each other in showing devotion to Israel. And recall how Prime Minister Benjamin Netanyahu of Israel humiliated the US president, Barack Obama, in 2015, by addressing both houses of Congress (to multiple standing ovations and without White House involvement) to campaign against Obama's nuclear deal with Iran. It's undeniable that since the events of May 2021, the attitude of the US body politic toward Israel has shifted, but the majority is still very supportive of Israel and reticent to criticize its actions.

The pro-Israel lobby works to ensure that the perception of "shared values" remains prevalent, and that the Jewish community continues to be highly engaged and speaks, largely, with one effective, unequivocal voice. Anything threatening these two pillars of pro-Israel advocacy is seen as a threat (to Israel, to self) and needs to be crushed.

A case in point is when Palestinian groups and their allies started accusing Israel of being an "apartheid state." A campus group at the

University of Toronto in 2005 established an activity they called Israeli Apartheid Week, which ran annually and spread to some fifty-five cities around the world. To Jews, comparing Israel to apartheid South Africa was a direct threat to the legitimacy of Israel and, therefore, they aimed to destroy it.

To achieve that goal, Jewish organizations claimed Jewish students attending university campuses that ran the Apartheid Week activities felt unsafe. Pressure was put on campus administrations to ban the activity, but most didn't, citing the necessity for free expression and thought in academia. Pressure was applied to politicians, who complied; from then-prime minister of Canada Steven Harper to the leader of the opposition, Michael Ignatieff, to members of the Toronto city council and its mayor, Rob Ford. They all condemned Apartheid Week as divisive, dangerous, ignorant, antisemitic, hateful—or a variation on the above. (For a more detailed account of events on college campuses, see *The Conflict Over the Conflict: The Israel/Palestine Campus Debate* by Kenneth Stern.)

While the Palestinian groups won the free speech academic battle, the political establishment denounced their efforts and gave them a public face associated with hate and intolerance. Instead of creating sympathy for the suffering of Palestinians living under occupation, the public view slanted towards concern for the safety of the Jewish students on campus. This is how mainstreamed muscularity further marginalizes Palestinian resistance: it crushes it.

Frustration, disempowerment, and marginalization lead to radicalization. Someone without a voice turns to insults. Anger over being silenced (by accusations of antisemitism) turns to outbursts of frustration. This is how the interplay between muscularity contributes to the marginalization of Palestinian resistance. This is what lashing out at the political elites who choose winners and losers looks like. And it gets us nowhere.

Some Palestinians deny that Jews are a people and therefore are undeserving of self-determination and statehood. They see Judaism as a religion (which they have no quarrel with) and not as a unique culture or ethnicity. It is their way of negating the legitimacy of

Zionism. And it is a misguided way. Denying the peoplehood of a group that sees itself as a people is wrong. It should be evident that Jews are a people that historically lived in the land called Palestine[45] until the Romans pushed them into exile.

For their part, many Zionist leaders have long denied the existence of Palestinians as a people. From the phrase "a land without a people for a people without a land," associated with early Zionists in reference to Palestine, to the proclamation in June 1969 by then-prime minister Golda Meir that "there were no such thing as Palestinians," many Zionists have acted as if no one was displaced when Israel was created since there was no one there to displace.

Meir also said, "It was not as though there was a Palestinian people in Palestine considering itself as a Palestinian people, and we came and threw them out and took their country away from them. They did not exist." While an Israeli prime minister today will not repeat these words, the living reality of Palestinians and the ongoing theft of their land is premised on them being essentially an inconvenient reality—that one can pretend didn't exist.

Peace movements in Israel-Palestine and the Diaspora have always recognized and accepted the Other as a necessary way of moving toward coexistence. Listening to the Other's narrative and understanding it are essential components for those who genuinely seek an end to the struggle between Jews and Palestinians—over there and over here.

PALESTINIAN RESISTANCE – SOME HISTORY

Palestinian resistance did not start with the occupation of 1967, but in the early days following the end of World War I.

There was general Arab disappointment at the abandonment of the promise of independence, which was given to them by the British during the war. Further, Palestinians believed the Balfour Declaration meant the denial of their right to self-determination and feared increased European Jewish migration would lead to eventual economic and political subjugation by the Jews. If a specific date were to be put on the start of Palestinian resistance, November 2, 1918—which is when nonviolent protests marked the first anniversary of the Balfour Declaration—would be a good candidate.

There were riots, clashes, and revolts throughout the British Mandate, culminating with the 1947–48 wars and the Nakba. Palestinians who were able to stay in Israel when the state was created lived formally under military rule from 1948 until the end of 1966.

Those who ended up in neighboring countries would eventually start organizing, and, in 1959, the Palestinian National Liberation Movement (later renamed Fatah) was formed as a political movement by Palestinian professionals working in the Arab Gulf countries, among them Yasser Arafat. In 1965 Fatah became a political party, and, following the Six-Day War in 1967, it joined the Palestine Liberation Organization and became the dominant force in Palestinian politics.

The PLO had been established at an Arab League summit in 1964 to "liberate Palestine and achieve Palestinian self-determination." Its first meeting took place in East Jerusalem, on May 28, 1964, when 422 Palestinian representatives met to elect a leader, Ahmed Shuqeiri, set up a legislative body, the Palestinian National Council (PNC), the PLO Executive Committee, a National Fund, and the Palestine Liberation Army (PLA).[46]

The PLO backed the use of armed struggle to achieve its goals. After the end of the Six-Day War, various factions of the PLO commenced guerrilla operations against Israeli forces inside the occupied West Bank, using the east bank of the Jordan River as a staging ground. Following clashes with the Jordanian army in 1970, the PLO was forced out of Jordan and made its way to Lebanon, where it resumed its attacks on Israel from the south of the country.

On October 14, 1974, the United Nations General Assembly recognized the PLO as the "sole legitimate representative of the Palestinian people," and on October 28, 1974, the League of Arab States followed suit. Following the 1982 Israeli invasion of Lebanon and the siege of Beirut, the PLO was exiled to Tunisia, 2,000 kilometers away from Israel's borders.

On November 15, 1988, the PLO declared Palestinian independence from its base in Tunisia, and the following month recognized the existence of Israel in its 1967 borders and renounced terrorism. In 1993, Israel recognized the PLO as the legitimate representative of the Palestinian people, as part of the Oslo Accords.

These agreements came largely as the result of the first intifada, which started in December 1987 and lasted until September 1993. This popular uprising came as a reaction to intensified Israeli land expropriation, increased settlement construction in the West Bank and Gaza, and the emergence of new grassroots Palestinian activists who questioned the leadership of the PLO. Most of the protests pitted rock-throwing Palestinian teenagers against armed Israeli soldiers firing rubber-coated bullets and, at times, live ammunition. In more violent scenarios, young Palestinian men throw Molotov cocktails and hand grenades at Israeli armored vehicles. But the images splashed on TV screens around the world were mostly of the rock-throwing variety, reminding everyone, including Israelis, that Palestinians continue to live under an oppressive occupation, one that they are increasingly prepared to resist. This proved to be so politically and economically damaging to Israel that a new government was elected in 1992 with a mandate to negotiate for peace.

At the same time, after being pushed out of Lebanon and into exile in Tunisia in 1982, the PLO had felt increasingly isolated and in no control of the intifada and its grassroots leadership—the main events occurring on the ground. So, when the Norwegian government sought secret talks to explore peace options between Israel and the PLO, it found welcoming ears. While offering a framework for a peace process meant to culminate with a peace agreement within five years, repeated failures of the process, accompanied by frustrations and mutual recriminations, led to a second intifada that was far more violent than the first.

Between 1993 and 2000, a newly organized force came to the fore in the Palestinian territories that rejected the Oslo Accords and sought the establishment of an Islamic state in all of historic Palestine. Hamas quickly resorted to the suicide bombing of civilian targets in an attempt to scuttle peace talks. All the while, Israeli settlement construction and expansion continued, as did land expropriations.

The election of Ariel Sharon as prime minister in 2001, followed by his provocative visit to the Al Aqsa Mosque/Temple Mount, sparked the second intifada.

By 2005, after much violence and devastation, tight controls had been placed on the movement of Palestinian goods and people, stifling their economy. The Israeli peace camp had all but disappeared, and the shift to the right of a large majority of Israeli society was complete. The separation wall was going up around and into the West Bank, Yasser Arafat had passed away, settlements were continuing to grow, and prospects for peace looked very dim. Amid all these failures and widely held perceptions of corruption, Palestinians, out of sheer frustration, voted for a Hamas majority in the legislature in 2006.

The wall and a security agreement between Israel and the Palestinian Authority, which remained in control of the West Bank, ensured that suicide bombings would end, and violent Palestinian resistance emanating from the West Bank would be kept to a minimum.

Hamas's election win, followed by its forceful takeover of power in Gaza in 2007, prompted a harsh blockade by Israel, assisted by Egypt, that continues until today. A number of wars have since been waged on Gaza, known in Israeli parlance as the periodic need to "mow the lawn."[47]

In an opinion piece in the Jewish News Syndicate, columnist Ariel Ben Solomon states, "The question is whether Israel used enough force in Operation Protective Edge in 2014 and inflicted enough pain on the enemy to purchase a sizeable chunk of time as respite before the next round of 'grass mowing.'"[48] The view of Palestinian resistance in Gaza as something that needs to be mowed down every once in a while, completely negates and disregards the humanity of the nearly two million people who live there.

Yet this is exactly what propaganda has succeeded in doing: equating Gaza with Hamas and terrorism. When Israeli F-16s, missiles, and bombs flatten entire neighborhoods in Gaza, the families and livelihoods being decimated are not what enters into public consciousness. Israel's supporters only see terrorist threats to Israel being "mowed down." Palestinian supporters, on the other hand, are thinking of the families and schools and hospitals being obliterated. To them, Israel's supporters look callous and indifferent to the loss of Palestinian lives. And when they object, Israel's supporters see them as sympathizers of Hamas—and terrorism.

NONVIOLENT RESISTANCE

I choose to be Palestinian
I can
because my identity is my own to create
It is no one's business
to affirm, prescribe, or bestow upon me
No need to defend my identity
because it comes from within;

I choose to be Palestinian
Not a box to check, a club to join,
or "lifestyle demographic,"
trust me

I choose to be Palestinian
and it has nothing to do with my ancestry
I choose to be Palestinian
because I believe in dignity,
in justice and humanity,
in perseverance,
in resilience...
Say it, Palestinian!

—Dana Dajani

Can a poem, a play, a dress, a film, or a cookbook be a form of resistance? A better question may be: is an affirmation of Palestinian identity and culture an act of defiance? Many Palestinians have taken to the arts and literature to affirm their connection to their culture as an act of, if not defiance, then resilience. They recreate forms of their culture as a means to claim and preserve them. They celebrate their identity in order to affirm it.

Take food, for instance. Palestinians get incensed when what they know as their food gets promoted in restaurants and cookbooks internationally as "Israeli food." It represents to them an erasure of existence and an appropriation of their culture by the same forces that have dispossessed and made them foreigners in their own land.

Reem Kassis, author of *The Palestinian Table* (2017), wrote an article in *The Washington Post* titled "Here's why Palestinians object to the term 'Israeli food': It erases us from history."[49] In it she writes, "Food, after all, is an expression of history, culture and tradition. By this token, presenting dishes of Palestinian provenance as 'Israeli' not only denies the Palestinian contribution to Israeli cuisine, but it erases our very history and existence."

In an interview published in *Haaretz*, the well-known Palestinian chef and author Sami Tamimi said, "I agree with that statement. Talking about an 'Israeli' kitchen erases my Palestinian identity, and there is no doubt that it is cultural appropriation ... when the stronger side claims exclusivity and brings about the disappearance of the weak side."[50] He adds, "What really irks me are some of the Israeli chefs who market the food as Israeli and take credit for it themselves."

Ronit Vered, the food reporter interviewing Tamimi writes, "In Israeli culture, which for years has refused to acknowledge the fact that in the relations with the Palestinians we who have the upper hand, the word 'Palestine' is still a red flag." She adds, "The word 'Palestinian' still sticks in the craw and is unacceptable to a large public who do not recognize the existence of the Palestinian identity or consider it a threat to Israeli identity and existence."

This "food fight" is clearly about a lot more than hummus and falafel. In recent years, a number of Palestinian chefs have responded by publishing their own recipes that are certifiably Palestinian by virtue of the stories and traditions that accompany them. These books include *The Gaza Kitchen: A Palestinian Culinary Journey* (2013), by Laila el-Haddad and Maggie Schmitt; *Palestine on a Plate* (2016) and

Baladi: Palestine (2018), by Joudie Kalla; and *Zaitoun: Recipes and Stories from the Palestinian Kitchen* (2018), by Yasmin Khan.

It would appear that the more Israeli society is reluctant to name the food they love so much—which they call Mizrahi, a term denoting Jews of Arabic descent—as Palestinian, and as long as Israeli chefs appropriate Palestinian cuisine as their own, the more likely it is that Palestinians will continue to reclaim and defend their food. They will continue to resist the erasure of their culture and identity by other means.

Similarly, in the world of fashion, Palestinians accuse high-end Israeli designers of appropriating traditional Palestinian fabrics and designs into their couture.[51] Palestinian fashion designer Haya Khalid says her motivation to create her own brand (ReBorn) of modern Palestinian fashion came from the "other side of the wall." She's referring to Israeli designer Yaron Minkowski's participation in Tel Aviv Fashion Week in 2015,[52] with a line of garments fabricated out of the kaffiyeh, the traditional checkered scarf that has come to symbolize Palestinian nationalism, a move that many Palestinians found offensive.

In 2016, a line of dresses and miniskirts sold at the chic stores owned by actress-designer Dorit Baror[53] in Tel Aviv, also made out of kaffiyeh, drew accusations of cultural appropriation and the "eroticization" of the Palestinian "symbol of resistance."[54] While Minkowski's use of the kaffiyeh was meant as a gesture of outreach to Palestinian culture, it failed to recognize the power dynamics at play: between those who have lost so much and are holding on to their identity and culture by a thread, and those who feel entitled to employ symbols that do not belong to them in their work.

Many North American and European cities host annual Palestinian film festivals that show features, shorts, and documentaries by and about Palestinians. They tend to be well-executed and well attended. Palestinian films have been nominated for Academy Awards, Golden Globes, and other prestigious awards—although not without controversy. Given that Palestine is not officially recognized as a state by the United Nations, and in an act of defiance to that technicality, many of these film festivals have used the name Palestine (instead of the more grammatically appropriate Palestinian) in their names, including the Toronto Palestine Film Festival, Reel Palestine Film Festival, Bristol Palestine Film Festival, and Boston Palestine Film Festival.

Spoken-word poetry from young Palestinian women like Dana Dajani (excerpted above) and Rafeef Ziadeh has attracted young audiences on social media and in cities around the Diaspora. Their poetry is empowered and assertive in projecting a positive and resilient Palestinian identity. In the face of dubious and malevolent accusations that Palestinians teach their children to hate, in 2011, Ziadeh released her poem "We teach life, sir," which went viral.

In order to remind the world of the humanity of the people of Gaza (or that Gaza does not equal Hamas), the Gaza-born Palestinian-Canadian-Australian Samah Sabawi wrote and mounted a play, *Tales of a City by the Sea*. The play is about "life and love in the besieged Gaza strip," and is "a story of human survival and tenacity." Set during the 2008–09 bombing campaign of Gaza, it ironically premiered during the 2014 war on Gaza, and has since toured many cities around the world and won several awards.

Perhaps the mother of all forms of nonviolent Palestinian resistance is the Boycott, Divestment, and Sanctions movement that we discussed in Chapter 4. To young Palestinians in the Diaspora, BDS provides a way in which they can connect with their identity, express support for the Palestinian cause, and be part of a community that rejects the continued oppression of Palestinians. It is a peaceful way to express a political opinion that has taken root at many North American and European college campuses, sparking what has been called the campus wars. Many Jewish students have been convinced that BDS is antisemitic and feel threatened when they encounter BDS supporters.

Israel's supporters claim that one of the pillars of the BDS movement, "Respecting, protecting and promoting the rights of Palestinian refugees to return to their homes and properties as stipulated in UN resolution 194," is antisemitic. The right of return, as it has been known, is highly problematic for Zionists. In their thinking, a return of all Palestinian refugees and their descendants to what used to be their homes in historic Palestine would reduce the country's Jews to a minority, thereby wiping out Israel as a Jewish state. And, as we said before, Zionists believe Israel's existence is necessary to prevent another Holocaust from happening. Palestinians need to understand that Jews truly believe this.

The logic that follows is a zero-sum, linear equation: Israel is an expression of self-determination of the Jewish people. If you are in favor of the right of return, it means you are for the destruction of Israel as a Jewish-majority state and against the Jewish right to self-determination. This has to mean you are antisemitic.

A Palestinian would scoff at such an assertion, saying something like, "I just want to be able to go back to the village my parents and entire ancestry are from. Your need for Jewish majority is none of my concern. I had no part in the Holocaust or the oppression you experienced in Europe. I don't hate Jews and just want my homeland back."

And herein lies the crux of the struggle: the zero-sum-ness of the logic followed by both sides. The two-state solution was supposed to provide a way for sharing the land that met each side's aspiration for self-determination. Almost three decades since Oslo, it has yet to happen, and the strength of the settler/annexation movement suggests that it never will. Can Jews and Palestinians, at least in the Diaspora, imagine a nonlinear formula for relating to the Other, free from deeply ingrained tropes, equally respectful of both peoples, principled in human rights and the equality of rights?

Can Zionists recognize that everything Zionism has given to the Jews (land, self-determination, identity, security), it has taken away from Palestinians? Can Palestinians recognize that wishing Zionists away and back to Europe will not return things to the way they were in old Palestine?

PART III – HARDENING THE WALL: WEAPONIZING THE NARRATIVE

"The bamboo that bends is stronger than the oak that resists."
—Japanese proverb

CHAPTER 7
JEWISH EXCEPTIONALISM AND PALESTINIAN OTHERNESS

"I may not have been sure about what really did interest me,
but I was absolutely sure about what didn't."
—Albert Camus, *The Stranger*

We have laid out a case for how we, in society as a whole, and Jews and Palestinians specifically, have been indifferent to the Other, their narrative, and even their most basic concerns. We have pointed to several reasons why they have become so distant from those with whom they, particularly in terms of their shared traumatic pasts, have much in common. This includes our natural inclination to "confirming information," our filtering system that repels uncomfortable learning, and our conflation of history itself with our memory of our own personal and tribal history. We have named three specific culprits ("mortar in the wall") that exacerbate our natural tendency to resist knowledge that challenges our preconceived notions of ourselves and of the Other: identity, trauma, and victimhood. We then described in depth how these phenomena play out in three specific discourses: antisemitism, Zionism and the Nakba, and Palestinian resistance.

To this point, we have looked at phenomena that Palestinians and Jews tend to see antithetically. While what has happened and is still happening over there is very important to understanding the polarization between Jews and Palestinians in the two Diasporas, we also need to understand the vast difference in how these are seen in Western society as a whole.

Like Bashir and Goldberg, we recognize that the two metanarratives, the Holocaust and the Nakba, resonate in every corner of the struggle today. However, we need to question why one has penetrated the psyche of the West and one has not. One is ubiquitous and the other is rarely spoken about. Why is support for Israel the default position in mainstream thinking in the West, particularly in the United States and Canada? Why are negative stories of Arabs so easily and fully absorbed into the North American discourse? Why are statements of concern for Palestinians often met with accusations of antisemitism? How have these ways of thinking led to the adoption of the IHRA definition by so many institutions and governmental systems?

The Israel-Palestine discourse in North America takes place not only within the Jewish and Palestinian communities but within society and its institutions at large.

Identity, trauma, and victimhood, within the two Diasporas, can be largely explained by how the two communities carry their family stories of trauma and victimhood with them. The effects of inter-generational trauma and the resulting victimhood are an important part of the wall between. This contributes greatly to trapping many progressive Jews in a nether space between being advocates for Palestinian rights and fighting against the scourge of antisemitism.

For liberal Jews, the challenge often seems that they frame their activism within a "pro-Israel, pro-peace" paradigm (self-determina-tion for both Jews and Palestinians: a two-state solution). This allows them to call out injustice perpetrated by the Israeli government but greatly limits their ability to be seen as leaders in a nuanced discussion about Israel-Palestine, as the ugly monster of antisemitism is never too distant in their rearview mirror. Israel, in spite of many concerns, is not only a spiritual homeland for many Jews, but a necessity for Jewish safety, or at least for the Jewish psyche. Rather than remain focused on human rights for all, these groups often call out Palestinian activism, including BDS, seeing it as a threat to Israel and therefore a threat to Jewish safety. The key here is to resist seeing trauma as only "ours" and instead focus on the pain that it causes, not just to us but to the Other.

The discourse on antisemitism also plays out in a broader socio-political context that engages both the Left and Right. They both fight it but blame a different enemy. For the Left, white supremacists are the main drivers of antisemitism. For the Right, the Left itself is to blame. The Right sees criticism of Israel coming from leftist academics and activist movements such as BDS that, in their view, unfairly target Israel for criticism. As a result, despite vast differences in approach to the topic of Israel/Palestine, the fixation with antisemitism, driven by a concern for Jewish safety and thus the necessity for Israel, propels the discourse, not Palestinian human rights and freedoms.

What we really need to tackle here is why so many non-Jews in the West seem naturally pre-disposed to the pro-Israel narrative. Jews today are seen, to a large degree, as an integral part of Western society, but this was not the case until relatively recently—how did this shift happen?

The historical reality of both the United States and Canada is the consistent and unrelenting presence of antisemitism. This has not only affected Jews but also society as a whole. In the time of greatest need, the governments of Canada and the United States not only did little to help but also actively obstructed those who were trying to shine a light on what was happening to the Jews in Europe.

Part of this can be explained by examining the immigration policies in both the United States and Canada, which tightened significantly in the early part of the twentieth century. In 1924, the US passed the Johnson-Reed Act, which greatly limited immigration from specific countries. Quotas were made that specified how many immigrants could come from a particular country, driven by those who were proponents of eugenics—seeing certain races as more desirable than others. While this greatly limited immigration of people from

Asian and African countries, many southern and eastern European Jews were also considered low on the desirability scale and therefore their quota was set very low. During this time, the United States had no refugee program enabling people to seek refuge from violent oppression. What was especially problematic for Jewish immigration was that the quotas were set by one's country of origin, not country of citizenship. Even though many Jews had emigrated from Eastern Europe to countries with high (US) quotas, like Great Britain and Germany, their country of origin (in Eastern Europe), which had very low quotas, blocked them from being able to take advantage of the favorable quota numbers of their adopted country of citizenship.[55]

The Johnson-Reed Act remained in place until 1965.

Similarly, in the early 1900s, Canada passed a series of immigration laws that limited immigration to Canada and focused on "desirable populations." In the Immigration Act of 1910, "immigrants determined to be 'unsuited to the climate or requirements of Canada' were prohibited."[56]

In their book, *None Is Too Many: Canada and the Jews of Europe, 1933–1948*, Irving Abella and Harold Troper lay out the case that Canada callously disregarded the plight of European Jews. The title of the book is a quote from an unidentified Canadian Immigration official who responded to a question inquiring how many Jews Canada should take in with the now-infamous phrase, "None is too many."

In 1938, representatives from thirty-two countries met in Evian, France, to explore solutions to the growing Jewish refugee crisis. Sadly, almost all countries in attendance refused to accept more Jews. Nicaragua, Costa Rica, Honduras, and Panama stated that "they wanted no traders or intellectuals," code words for Jews. Australia said that it had no "racial problems" and did not want to create any by bringing in Jewish refugees. The US said that only Congress could change immigration quotas, and Mackenzie King, the Canadian prime minister, said, "We must … seek to keep this part of the continent free from unrest and from too great an intermixture of foreign strains of blood."[57]

While other groups, most notably Japanese, Chinese, and people from many African countries were also greatly disadvantaged by US and Canadian immigration policies, the guilt that has remained in the Western ethos surrounding the limited immigration during the lead up to the Holocaust is a critical factor in understanding the often-unquestioned connection to Jews, and, by extension, to Israel.

Antisemitism rippled throughout North American society. In Canada, there were public places where Jews were not allowed and towns where they were not allowed to buy property. In the 1920s and 1930s, Jews were often seen as conspirators, particularly in the province of Quebec, where the view held that Jews wanted to dismantle the leadership of the Catholic Church. There were also quotas of how many Jews could attend universities in Quebec. Many Jews who grew up in the 1950s and 1960s, particularly in largely Catholic areas of Canada (mostly in Ontario and Quebec), remember dealing with daily antisemitic taunts, including physical threats.[58]

In the US, many prominent antisemites held positions of power, including Henry Ford, the founder of the Ford Motor Company. Jews in the US were also barred from attending certain universities, and the Klu Klux Klan often targeted Jews.

The recent rise in white supremacist-led antisemitic events—such as the march on Charlottesville, Virginia, where white supremacists carried tiki torches and chanted "Jews will not replace us," and two synagogue shootings, one in Pittsburgh, Pennsylvania, and the other in Poway, California—has also intensified the connection and empathy for the Jewish community that is prevalent in American society. While much of this is driven by anti-immigrant sentiment and conspiratorial theories of Jewish influence on government policies (as many Jewish groups are strong supporters of broader immigration policies) rather than religious or racial hatred for Jews, this nuance is frequently glossed over, but instead seen as an indication of growing Jew-hatred, by the right and the left.

The transformation in how Jews are viewed in Western society, from the immigration quotas of the early and mid-twentieth century, when Jews were firmly ensconced in "undesirable status," to today, where Jews are fully contributing members of society and visible in all areas of social, political, and commercial life, is truly remarkable. But the scars remain. The past and the present are blended rather than separated. The echoes of antisemitism linger, not just for Jews, but for Western society as a whole.

Identity plays such a prominent role in who is in and who is out, who we see as part of "us" and who we see as part of the Other. North Americans tend to see Israel in a positive light for many reasons, but perhaps most influential is how Jews today, to a very large degree, are sewn into the fabric of Western culture.

To understand the seismic shift in how Jews have come to be viewed, we can listen to how today's politicians talk compared to those of eighty years ago, at the time of the Evian conference. On the occasion of Israeli Independence Day in April 2021, Prime Minister Justin Trudeau of Canada stated:

> "Canada is proud to stand with Israel. We will continue to oppose efforts to isolate Israel internationally and to condemn BDS and any movement that attacks our Israeli friends, Jewish Canadians, and the values we share ... We also reaffirm our promise to fight antisemitism and hate wherever and whenever they occur, including through our support for the International Holocaust Remembrance Alliance's working definition of antisemitism, which we adopted as part of our anti-racism strategy."[59]

In this statement, he not only links Jewish values with Canadian values, he draws a direct link between support for the Jewish community in Canada and support for Israel. As is common in today's political discourse around Israel/Palestine, he goes further to link antisemitism with anti-Zionism (or even the hint of anti-Zionism).

Similarly, Democratic politicians in the US, known for raising the alarm about human rights violations, are almost ubiquitously supportive of Israel and resistant to Palestinian concerns. While a small group of progressive Democrats continue to challenge the status quo on Israel, most of their fellow lawmakers disregard this view.[60]

Another aspect of this view is that Jews are included in the racial construct of "whiteness." This, coupled with collective guilt over the Holocaust, appalling immigration policies, and a deep history of antisemitism in North America are important facets in understanding how Jews, and by extension Israel, are viewed empathetically in the United States and Canada. The vast majority of North American Jews are "white" in terms of their social status and privilege, although they may feel they are not fully included in the power framework of whiteness. Or they may feel this inclusion is offset to some degree by historical and current antisemitism. Many liberal academics, however, argue that Jews today benefit greatly from being seen as white and are ensconced in the upper levels of society, professionally, economically, and politically. This view, in itself, is seen by many as tainted by antisemitism, recalling old tropes of Jews using their power to control others.

Our point here is to show how the current status of Jews in mainstream society, unlike the Jewish experiences of the past, is by and large free from "othering." While fringes of Western society still hold virulently antisemitic views, including conspiratorial notions of Jews working together to destroy the fabric of Western society or to control the media, this is no longer the norm.

What may be most significant is how Jews are seen in contrast to Arabs, particularly Arab Muslims. In the section on identity, we discussed how you must have a "them" in order to create an "us." Importantly, this is largely a subliminal process that often does not require our consent.

Arabs have been seen as outsiders in Western society since the Crusades. Palestinian-American intellectual Edward Said wrote in his widely read tome *Orientalism,* "The Muslim orient was the only real threat to Christian Europe." The Islamic world, since medieval times, has conjured up feelings of contempt and fear in the Western mind. While views of the Muslim as a terrorist have become more commonplace since 9/11, Arabs have been painted with a singular brush for many millennia: the Brown menace that we must be leery of. While many liberal groups have pushed back against the stereotyping of Arabs, this has not eroded the general perception of Arabs in the West: "They" are not like "us."

As we will delve into more closely in Chapter 8, the otherness of Arabs has been operationalized by a finely tuned propaganda machine that plays on our fears, encouraging our worst instincts. While those deeply engaged in the Israel-Palestine discourse may have met a few Palestinians, Palestinians remain the "other Other." Arabs may be known at some level (think the bustling metropolis of Dubai or the ancient ruins of Egypt), but what interactions have most North Americans had with a Palestinian? Or how many works of literature by Palestinian writers or paintings by Palestinian artists have they been exposed to? To most people, Palestinians are likely no more than a sound-bite on the evening news or a leftist cause picked up by some fringe group, which, in itself, makes them more suspicious. For many, Palestinians are the militant Islamist behind rockets being launched at Sderot, or the suicide bomber who blew up Israeli buses and cafes.

Another element in the "us versus them" paradigm in the West is the rise of Christian Zionism. The idea of Christians supporting Jewish return to the biblical land of Israel is not new, tracing back to sixteenth-century England. However, the movement has grown greatly in the last forty or fifty years. Christian Zionism, at first blush, is a most unlikely interfaith movement. Adopted by many Evangelicals, whose own teaching suggests that Jews must convert to Christianity in order to be spared a terrible fate in the end times, Christian Zionism embraces Israel. This bond includes a close working relationship between Christian Zionists and ultra-orthodox settlers in the West Bank, who are in many ways, strange bedfellows, but a relationship that has served both groups nevertheless.

None of this would happen without the othering of Arabs, especially Arab Muslims. While Jews and Muslims have been historically positioned as a threat to Christianity, today the rift between Christians and Jews has been largely healed, but the demonization of Arab Muslims has, in fact, increased.

The Trump administration's demonstrations of loyalty to Israel, including moving the US Embassy to Jerusalem, were done in large part to court the Evangelical vote. While the alliance between Christian evangelicals and Israel is driven by an affinity for Jews, it also stems from an intolerance for Islam.

Antisemitism, while certainly still evident in small pockets of right- and left-wing extremism, is not the pervasive problem that the pro-Israel lobby paints it as, politicizing antisemitism to prop up support for Israel and defuse Palestinian voices.

This has sadly not occurred for anti-Arabism. The gulf between how Jews and Arabs are viewed in the West cannot really be overstated in understanding why the discourse tends to be so one-sided. Many Palestinians and their supporters now cite the differential treatment given to Israel that ignores human rights abuses against Palestinians as a prime example of anti-Palestinian racism.

Israel also benefits from how it is modeled after European and North American liberal democracies. This creates a natural bond between Israel and Israelis and the West. Israel is seen as a direct contrast to many Muslim-dominant countries that are viewed monolithically as theocratic states, founded on a distinctly "foreign" ideology that is generally seen as antithetical to "Western values."

All of this contributes to the general reluctance to look deeply at what is happening in Israel-Palestine, no less to hold Israel accountable for its policies and actions. We argue that Jewish trauma and victimhood have reverberated throughout Western society. As we have laid out here, this has evolved from a combination of guilt over historical antisemitism, the feeling that Jews, generally, are part of "us," and distrust of Arabs in general and Islam specifically. The trauma of 9/11 has contributed to the gulf between "us" and "them." In short, the support for Jews and the support for Israel have become so woven together that it is hard to distinguish one from the other.

The question we are answering in the following chapters is, How do we make this shift from a discourse framed within our tribal alliances to a justice-driven discourse? How do we break free from the bonds formed through identity, trauma, and victimhood (ITV) and embrace values-forward thinking (VFT)? In Chapter 8, we hone in on how sophisticated propaganda machines manipulate our ITV to weaponize tribalism. In Chapter 9, we chart the path to a discourse that rejects ITV thinking and replaces it with VFT. This shift, we argue, is the only way out of the endless cycle of blame and recrimination.

CHAPTER 8
WEAPONIZING TRIBALISM

*"You can sway a thousand men by appealing to their prejudices
quicker than you can convince one man by logic."*
—Robert A. Heinlein

WHAT IS THE TRUTH? DOES IT MATTER?

These are questions worth asking in the age of "alternative facts" and "stolen elections," when the dismissal of truth is threatening the very foundations of the "world's greatest democracy." To be sure, propaganda has existed since the beginning of time. Rhetoric has justified wars, atrocities, and genocide. Hitler's propaganda machine was notorious for instigating and rationalizing the unimaginable.

It's been said that truth is the first casualty of war—for good reason. It is hard to make the case for war, the killings, and the atrocities it is bound to unleash. Governments create compelling narratives that describe threats so terrifying that war appears as a regrettable yet necessary evil—undesirable, yet unavoidable. "Weapons of mass destruction." "The communist menace." "Another 9/11." "Terrorists." "We have to kill them before they kill us."

It's also been said that history is written by the victor. In other words, the truth is on the side of the one left standing. For a long time, our truth was that the indigenous peoples of North America were barbarous "Indian" savages whose only intent was to kill decent, civilized, white Europeans. The enemy is always dehumanized in order to create an appetite for slaughter, and for history to be told the way it needs to be.

In the age of anything-goes internet, social media "vomitoriums," and "deepfake" apps, truth has become harder to decipher and easier to dismiss. Which means, it really matters.

Of course, propaganda, newspeak, agitprop, disinformation, counterinformation, indoctrination, hype—you name it—have played a big part in the Israel-Palestine story since before there was an Israel. "Palestine is a land without a people for a people without a land," is a statement often associated with early Zionist settlers. How else can one explain the similarity of perceptions that most in the Palestinian and Jewish Diaspora communities have of each other and the struggle in Israel-Palestine? That each community holds what it sees as undisputable, undeniable, universal truths about the Other? That tribal thinking, and only tribal thinking, is acceptable in respectable company on each side?

Tribal thinking in the Jewish community tends to hold the following beliefs:

- The Arabs are out to kill us. They are the new Nazis; they hate Jews.
- Israel does what it does because it has to protect the Jewish people.
- The Wall, the Gaza blockade, etc., are "necessary evils" for security.
- We are the one lone democracy in the region—why are you always picking on us?
- Had the Arabs accepted the partition plan, the Palestinians could have stayed in their homes; it was the Arabs who attacked Israel.
- Palestinians are waging war on Israel.
- Israel faces an existential threat on a daily basis.

Tribal thinking in the Palestinian community tends to hold the following beliefs:

- Everything that Israel does is evil and malicious.
- Zionism is pure racism; Zionists should be shunned completely.
- Israel wants to control the entire Middle East.
- All (OK, the overwhelming majority) of Jews support Israel no matter what.
- The media is sympathetic to Israel; Jews control the media.
- Jews are the source of all our miseries.
- If Israel does something good, it's only for public relations purposes.

Aside from demonstrating the complete distrust, if not outright animosity, between the communities, that such standard views are ubiquitous shows that many are singing from the same song sheets— and the name of the song is propaganda.

BADD ACTORS

Is propaganda a bad thing? Consider the many groups whose sole function is to find or concoct reasons to lay **B**lame on the Other, **A**ttack their actions, **D**emonize their intentions, and **D**ismiss their narrative. We call these groups BADD actors. Truth is most often irrelevant to such groups, since their job is to vilify. Their last motivation is integrity.

In going back to the wall between, and while it is kept together by the "mortar" of identity, trauma, and victimhood, we find that it has been hardened, fortified, and enclosed with "barbed wire" by the relentless bombardment of siloed information and misinformation: propaganda.

Of course, this is true for both Jews and Palestinians. But as we reinforce throughout the book, the pro-Israel information system hugely outweighs the Palestinian one in numbers, financial capacity, and political influence (e.g., AIPAC in the US and CIJA in Canada).

These propaganda machines are no minor obstacle to dismantling the wall between the sides and capitalizing on the "justice moment" that we are in. We have pointed to many examples in our chapters on antisemitism, Zionism and the Nakba, and Palestinian resistance, but this is just a small sampling. The pro-Palestinian and pro-Israel propaganda engines rely on us not engaging in critical thinking, rather to believe them at face value. They trigger our woundedness, presenting themselves as the only true protectors of their respective tribes. They reignite our trauma and perpetuate our victimhood.

Perpetuating Jewish victimhood is a bedrock tactic of the ever-expanding pro-Israel machinery of organizations in North America. Central to this tactic is the belief that when you see yourself as a victim, the only victim, you are not likely to see or be concerned with who you might be victimizing.

In order to control the narrative, these organizations regularly poke the wound of antisemitism to prevent it from healing, thus feeding, and growing historical fears. They dabble in anti-Palestinian tropes ("They teach their children to hate us") to keep the community on its toes, in fear of the Other, and in search of safety among its own. The persistent belief among many Jews in the Diaspora—that another Holocaust is going to happen and only Israel can prevent it—had to have been intentionally fostered.

The place that Jews hold in the world today, and in the West particularly, as a completely integrated part of the social system and its elite classes, in particular, would largely preclude such a possibility. The Holocaust was the culmination of centuries of systemic European antisemitism. While antisemitism, in some parts of the world, particularly in Eastern Europe, remains a serious concern, it is not systematized nor legitimized in the way it was in the pre-Holocaust world. Where it matters most in the power centers of the world (the West), antisemitism is categorically rejected. One cannot make a credible argument that antisemitism is embedded in Western governmental or societal systems, particularly when the IHRA definition of antisemitism has been so ubiquitously supported.

Yet many pro-Israel groups continue to promote the notion that antisemitism is always on the rise, and a "new antisemitism" has taken place under the guise of criticizing Israel.[61] In other words, there's no less antisemitism today, it has just changed its colors.

Most pro-Palestinian groups, on the other hand, reject the idea of Zionism utterly and unequivocally, promoting the notion that it is nothing but a settler-colonial, racist enterprise, that Judaism is a religion and not an ethnicity, and Jews are not a people; therefore, Jews do not have the right to self-determination.

Yet, if Israel had been formed on land other than Palestine, Palestinians would not have resorted to such arguments, or even bothered to concern themselves with the nature of Judaism, let alone the purpose of Zionism. What they do is a result of political arguments (propaganda) employed following 1948 in an effort to discredit Zionism, the force that caused their Nakba.

At times, Palestinian groups in the Diaspora manifest the victimhood of Palestinians to the point of paralysis. When Palestinians spend so much energy demonstrating and accentuating their victimhood and what Israel has done and continues to do to them, they end up capable of nothing more than *being* victims.

The problem of course is that victimhood removes your responsibility and puts it into the hands of others: the UN, the US, even Israel. The Palestinian leadership has traditionally been ineffective in defending and promoting their cause, focusing on "Israel is bad" and "Zionism is racism"—non-winning arguments in Western societies.

This is exacerbated by the reality that, like many other situations of disparities of power, the focus in North America became the response to abuses of power (such as BDS and Israel Apartheid Week) rather than the abuses themselves. Instead of the discourse being predominantly about Israeli abuses of Palestinian human rights, it was turned by slick and powerful propaganda into defending such protestations from accusations of antisemitism. Palestinians end up shadowboxing, defending their responses to power rather than talking about the abuses of power.

As an example, the Palestinian Authority (PA) and the United Nations Relief and Works Agency (UNRWA) have repeatedly faced accusations that Palestinian children's textbooks promote hatred of Jews (antisemitism) and incite violence. These accusations have been the subject of US congressional committee investigations, European Parliament resolutions, and UN condemnation. Palestinian textbooks have been repeatedly scrutinized by pro-Israel advocacy organizations, urging the defunding of the PA and UNRWA.

Yet, as Peter Beinart noted,[62] "the most comprehensive academic study, conducted by researchers from Yale, Tel Aviv and Bethlehem Universities, found that Israeli and Palestinian textbooks weren't dramatically different." The study in question, "Portrayal of the Other in Palestinian and Israeli Schoolbooks: A Comparative Study," [63] came to the conclusion that while "dehumanizing and demonizing characterizations of the Other are rare in both Israeli and Palestinian books; both Israeli and Palestinian books present unilateral national narratives that portray the Other as enemy."

In addition to defending themselves against charges of antisemitism, pro-Palestinian groups have long had to defend themselves against charges of supporting terrorism. A case in point is a lawsuit launched by the Jewish National Fund (JNF) against the Washington, DC-based organization US Campaign for Palestinian Rights (USCPR). The plaintiff argued that the "USPCR aided and abetted acts of 'international terrorism' by supporting the Great March of Return and the BDS National Committee (BNC)."[64] While the lawsuit failed, it showed the extent to which intimidation tactics are used to demonize and dismiss pro-Palestinian voices. (The Great March was a civilian response to the US's move of its embassy to Jerusalem, and BDS is a nonviolent form of protest against Israeli human rights abuses, as explained earlier.)

Zionists have long understood that they needed to win the narrative argument—convince Diaspora Jews and Western governments that Israel was justified in its actions, that Palestinians were the aggressors and Israelis the victims. *Hasbara*, a Hebrew word meaning "public relations efforts to defend abroad the point of view and policies of the State of Israel,"[65] has been a substantial component of Israel's foreign policy efforts for decades.

An entire "Ministry of Hasbara" was established in 1974, though it was later disbanded in favor of a multi-ministerial taskforce. "Since then, the importance of *hasbara* has come to the fore every time Israel has been involved in a major conflict," writes Yonatan Mendel in the *London Review of Books*. "Only the lack of efficient *hasbara*—and antisemitism—is allowed to explain the criticism Israel receives."[66] The ministry was reestablished in March 2009, two months after the invasion of Gaza of 2008–2009. Today, nearly 100 colleges in North America offer Hasbara Fellowships.

The tactic of presenting the victims as villains and the oppressors as the oppressed is effective. It was frequently used by former US president Donald Trump, such as when he called Black Lives Matter a "symbol of hate" while speaking out against the removal of Confederate emblems, thereby marginalizing the oppressed group and making them into the villains. The video showing wealthy white homeowners Mark and Patricia McCloskey pointing guns at Black Lives Matter demonstrators passing by their house in St. Louis, Missouri, suggests that at least some people bought into Trump's rhetoric. And when Israel, supported by the US and much of the West, requires Palestinians, the people it occupies, to provide it with security, it is clear that the same tactic has also worked for Israel.

GAZA = HAMAS?

The fourth "Gaza War," in May 2021, came with many firsts. The conflagration of violence between Israel and Palestinian protesters, which was followed by a confrontation between Israel and Hamas in Gaza, was initially sparked by attempts to evict Palestinians from their homes in the Sheikh Jarrah neighborhood of Jerusalem. Having experienced dispossession at the hands of Israelis since 1948, Palestinians everywhere reacted strongly to this latest attempt by Jewish settlers to displace yet more Palestinians from their homes.

The first first: Violence erupted between Jewish and Palestinian citizens of Israel living in "mixed" Israeli cities as Palestinians and their supporters around the world erupted in mass demonstrations demanding an end to the evictions. Palestinian citizens of Israel then joined Palestinians in the West Bank, Gaza, and East Jerusalem in an unprecedented general strike.

The second first: Hamas flexed its muscles with repeated barrages of missiles into Israeli cities, so massive that the Iron Dome missile defense system could not keep up, and a number of missiles landed on targets across the country, killing twelve civilians.

The third first: Hamas chose to enter a conflict that was not aimed at Gaza, rather in reaction to the events in Jerusalem, positioning itself as the defender of Palestinians, and scoring a major blow to the PA that sat complacent in its headquarters in Ramallah as events unfolded around it. No longer known just as Hamas, Palestinians came to refer to it as the Resistance.

The fourth first: The mainstream media in the West, likely influenced by real-time social media coverage of the war, paid a lot more attention to the Palestinian side of events than it usually does. Traditionally more sympathetic to the Israeli narrative, the mainstream media provided a more balanced approach and ample coverage of the civilian casualties and the damage to infrastructure caused by Israel's bombardment of Gaza. Commentators openly criticized the disproportionate use of power by Israel and questioned its appeasement of extremist settlers whose primary intent is to Judaize East Jerusalem.

The fifth first: And perhaps the most important one, justice movements in North America, such as Black Lives Matter[67] and Idle No More[68] in Canada, spoke out in defense of Palestinian rights and called for an end to Israeli abuses. Live coverage of the destruction in Gaza shared on social media was proliferated by racial justice activists, many of whom made prominent after the Black Lives Matter protests, and by the larger justice movement (including environmentalists) in the US. This shift in consciousness among North American progressives with regard to Israel-Palestine provided an uncommon "mainstreaming" of the righteousness of the Palestinian cause.

All of these firsts contributed to a swift end to the war, in eleven days, as compared to the seven weeks it took a similar conflagration in

2014 to end. The quick end was widely attributed to an unprecedented volume of appeals for intervention made to the US president, Joe Biden, by various progressive groups, non-government organizations, Democratic staffers and house representatives.[69] [70] [71] [72]

This didn't prevent mainstream Jewish organizations from (legitimately) condemning Hamas's indiscriminate rocket attacks while (spuriously) representing the conflict as solely between Hamas (a "terrorist organization") and Israel. It's easier to pick sides when you disregard the context of Hamas attacks: the threatened home evictions in Sheikh Jarrah, the subsequent attack on the Al Aqsa Mosque worshippers by Israeli police,[73] and the repeated clashes with young Palestinian men in Jerusalem.[74]

The "Gaza equals Hamas" strategy has always worked for pro-Israel organizations. When you mention Gaza to your average North American Jew, what comes to their mind is Hamas, not the nearly two million Palestinians living in some of the most squalid conditions on earth, due largely to Israel's yearslong blockade (with help from Egypt). Most Jews are so fully convinced of the evil of Hamas that the occasional mowing of the lawn is seen as a regrettable-yet-acceptable operation.

The Green Line, which separates Israel's internationally recognized borders from the West Bank, was made nearly invisible in May 2021 as the conflict spread to the entire areas controlled by Israel: Gaza, the West Bank, East Jerusalem, and Israel itself. The events demonstrated how Palestinians living anywhere "between the river and the sea" lacked justice and remained one people. The chant "From the river to the sea, Palestine will be free" was echoed by demonstrators around the world.

Typically, North American Jews, upon hearing such words, are reminded of the Holocaust and the possible loss of protection that Israel provides, when a Palestinian is thinking about their own freedom, not the annihilation of Jews. That freedom for Palestinians has been made into the equivalent of the destruction of Jews in the minds of many (a zero-sum game) is testimony to the power of propaganda and the dangers of unchallenged tribal thinking.

Clearly, much of our propaganda analysis in this chapter is focused on pro-Israel advocacy, and with good reason: it is impressive. Palestinian propaganda—from a newer and marginalized community in North America, comparatively under-resourced, and grossly outnumbered in size and scope—flails in comparison. Ours is not a stand against Israel, rather against the propaganda movement that prevents us from having an honest conversation about what has happened and what continues to happen.

In many ways, the picture we have painted of the present Israel-Palestine discourse in the West is fairly bleak. We have outlined how this has happened and, we trust, made the case for why it is necessary to change course. In the last section of the book, we make the case for a brighter and more hopeful discourse, one driven by "values-forward thinking." If you have been convinced that our discourse must change, or even if you already knew that, then Part IV is our partial remedy for the current toxicity in the struggle over here about the struggle over there.

PART IV – DISMANTLING THE WALL: THE MAKING OF A NEW NARRATIVE

CHAPTER 9
TOWARDS VALUES-FORWARD THINKING

"Never forget that justice is what love looks like in public."
—Cornel West

We have outlined how identity, trauma, and victimhood have created such polarization, both within the Jewish and Palestinian diasporas and Western society as a whole. We have also pointed out how BADD actors keep the trauma alive with constant reminders and hyperbolic language that blames, attacks, demonizes, and dismisses the Other. Perhaps the most important question now is, "So what?" What difference does any of this make? Have you, the reader, been influenced by what you have read? Is it possible that, at least with certain parts of the discourse, reading this book has only cemented your view of the Other and bolstered the surety that you hold the "right" positions? Or, might you have been exposed to the Other's thinking in a way that persuaded you to rethink your positions? Regardless of where you are at this moment, what is important is what comes next.

If you identify as a Jew or a Palestinian, or tend to side with one of these two groups, your position must not be cemented and, in fact, must include the concerns and needs of the other group for any change in the status quo to occur. Staying in our tribal camps has led to the intractable mess we are in. Contrary to typical thinking, the way out of this is not to simply become more empathetic, but to be freed from the tribal silo created by identity, trauma, and victimhood (ITV) and BADD behavior, which are responsible for the current cycle of belligerence and intractability. In the North American discourse, the better way forward is to shift our focus to Values-Forward Thinking (VTF), driven by our shared values of justice, dignity, and freedom.

One group views resistance as the only means to establishing their existence, while the other group views this resistance as a threat to their own existence. Zionism is life to one—and death to another. To one group, the events of 1948 symbolize redemption and are the answer to thousands of years of dislocation, oppression, and murder. But for the other, these same events represent the loss of everything— total dispossession, their greatest personal and existential tragedy. Antisemitism is an unrelenting attack on Jewish dignity and value, and a threat to Jews' survival. Yet, for Palestinians, it is the greatest weapon used against their resistance to their oppression. In today's stilted discourse, even a seemingly noncontroversial issue such as food becomes a cultural flashpoint.

We seem irreversibly trapped in a cycle of blame, a cycle that is entrenched by what is being fed to us every day, deepening our victimhood, scraping away at our open wounds, insisting that the only way forward is to win the war of ideas. This may be where we are, but it doesn't have to be where we remain. There is no "transporter" that can "beam" us out of this reality à la *Star Trek*, but there is a way to dematerialize from where we are now and rematerialize in a different world of our own creation.

The way forward requires rethinking our assumptions, moving through our identity-driven trauma, and rejecting the resulting victimhood.

This is a wake-up call.

We must be able to call out injustice without being labeled antisemitic. We must recognize the indelible scar the Holocaust has left on the Jewish psyche, while fairly separating Jewish trauma from the terrible consequences of 1948 and the current Occupation for Palestinians.

Now that you have read the first eight chapters of this book and understand better how the trifecta of ITV (identity, trauma and victimhood) has narrowed your worldview and limited your ability to see and respond empathetically to the Other, what will you do with this new learning? Recognizing how the plethora of propaganda has inserted itself into your traumatized brain, sank its fingers and twisted them inside your deep wounds, agitated your deeply ingrained victimhood, will you turn away from "confirming" information?

Common sense suggests we will do something productive with any new learning, but we don't always act from common sense, rather from habit. Our pattern-making brain has us react instinctively to what we hear. The knowledge we already have provides a safe cocoon, protected from the challenges created by transformative learning.

The "universal truths of tribal thinking" we refer to in Chapter 8 are examples of how we tend to stick with what we know rather than challenge it. When Jews are confronted with the consequences of 1948 for Palestinians, common thinking such as, "If they had only accepted the UN partition plan" or "They were the ones who attacked us" form a force-field around us, protecting us from taking in the painful learning we are being exposed to.

Similarly, when Palestinians hear stories from Jews about the Holocaust, their resentment over how the Holocaust has been, in their view, used as an excuse for 1948, they may be unable to absorb these stories.

Will we continue to respond with "Yes, but?" Will this book be another in the pile of pie-in-the-sky dreamings that gather dust on a high shelf? Or can each one of us begin, one step at a time, to disrupt the current discourse, to challenge the status quo, to not only engage with the Other, but to rethink their own existing narrative and become more invested in the Other's humanity?

The answer to this lies in how we chart the path from where we are now to where we need to be. The core pivot we are offering is to dismantle the wall by rejecting the cycle of blame and intransigence, convinced that we are the greater victims, and instead shift to values-forward thinking: being justice-centered, pushing forward rather than backward.

VALUES-FORWARD THINKING AND JUSTICE

Perhaps what is most challenging in how we talk about Israel-Palestine in the West is that we seem unable (or unwilling) to apply Western norms of human rights and dignity similarly for all the peoples involved in the struggle over there. Values-forward thinking is, in theory, a Western exceptionalist ideal. The United States in particular often uses its considerable clout to compel other nations to live up to the basic principles of universal rights and legal protections for all. This morally superior position, however, has rarely been used to push the Israeli government to treat Palestinians according to these same basic universal rights.

We have looked extensively at the causes for this phenomenon (including Jewish trauma, Western guilt, and geopolitical interests in the Middle East), but this is where we have been, not where we need to be. Among many definitions of "justice" in the Merriam-Webster Dictionary, the word is defined as the "establishment or determination of rights according to the rules of law or equity" and "the principle or ideal of just dealing or right action: conformity to this principle or ideal: righteousness."[75] The two drivers in this definition are the law and ethical principles—the backbones of both jurisprudence and Judeo-Christian ethics and moral theology in Western societies. And while the term "Judeo-Christian" traditionally refers to the shared values of Jews and Christians that govern Western thinking, it can also be a divisive term used to separate "real Americans" from immigrants who may adhere to other religious and/or cultural traditions.

A common pushback when Palestinian rights are brought to the forefront is that the right of the Jewish people to have safety and security matters first. This is similar to the response to Black Lives Matter that "all lives matter." The crux of this is that freedom for Palestinians is being falsely juxtaposed with a lessening of Jewish rights. Trauma is behind this but cannot continue to excuse us from squarely addressing the Occupation and other indignities, or wanting for Palestinians the same things we want for Jews. Our call for justice is based on the law and ethics. This is not anti-Israel and certainly not anti-Jewish but a reflection of the reality that learning about the Other and the injustice they suffer, and then failing to act to address it is, in itself, oppressive. Isn't the essence of supremacy preventing others from having the rights and privileges that you already have for yourself?

Being values-forward and justice-centered requires us to learn about the Other. Here, a Palestinian might respond with "Why should I want to understand my oppressor?" Or a Jew might query, "Why should I be concerned about Palestinian safety and security when it will compromise my own safety and security?" We reject this all-or-nothing thinking.

This book has clearly laid out that, while there are two narratives, there are not two equal sides, at least not in terms of power and ability to change the situation on the ground. This reality does not diminish the fact that in order for real change to occur, we have to deal with—and care for—each other.

"Care," a Palestinian would ask, "you want me to care for my oppressor?"

Establishing mutual interest is a part of any long-term peace process. Groups like Combatants for Peace (cfpeace.org), the Parents Circle-Families Forum (theparentscircle.org), Breaking the Silence (breakingthesilence.org), and B'Tselem (btselem.org) view care and concern for the trauma of the Other as essential. This does not diminish their concerns for systemic injustice but sees that the only real path forward is by caring for one another, focusing on mutual interest in ending the suffering of both peoples.

North American society as a whole needs to confront its biases without exchanging one set of biases for another. If pro-Israel thinking is simply replaced by anti-Israel thinking, what space is there for real, groundbreaking discourse and shared action? For example, working together to resist the Occupation is not in contest with concerns of Jews for safety and security (ITV), but these concerns cannot be used as an excuse for the Occupation, oppression, and total disenfranchisement of Palestinians (FVT).

We will name three specific paradigm shifts that can lead us from ITV to VTF: personalizing experiences of Jews and Palestinians, separating the past from the present, and rejecting groupthink.

FROM MANY TO ONE

We often think of great tragedies in terms of the number of people affected. In the two metanarratives at play in the Jewish-Palestinian discourse, the Holocaust and the Nakba, we think in terms of "six million Jews" murdered and "750,000 Palestinians" dispossessed.

The first step in humanizing such tragedies is to think of one Jew murdered six million times or one Palestinian exiled 750,000 times. In the Oscar-winning Holocaust drama *Schindler's List*, director Steven Spielberg repeatedly shows us a little girl in a red coat (the only color in an otherwise black-and-white film). Spielberg's aim seems to be for us to consider a single tragedy, and then multiply it six million times. The emotional impact of this is profound. Similarly, we have spoken throughout this book about the Other in monolithic terms: "Jews think," "Palestinians say," and so forth. While using these generalities is useful in painting a broad-stroked picture of how many people feel, the path forward is constructed one person at a time. The wall between must be dismantled brick by brick, conversation by conversation. We need to stop thinking of Jews and Palestinians as monoliths and instead engage one Jew and one Palestinian at a time. What if we were to not only think in terms of one Jew, six million times, or one Palestinian, 750,000 times, but we came to actually know that one person—cared for them, trusted them, and, over time, advocated for them?

Most, if not all of us, have experienced meeting someone who made personal our generalized thinking about a certain ethnic or religious group, or any group that we might narrowly define. The information machine cannot operate successfully if we begin to know and care about each other as individuals. Propaganda only works if the Other remains a monolith, one that by its sheer size and power can destroy us.

Once we begin to personalize trauma, we can multiply it. In other words, when we talk in terms of "six million" or "750,000" (or more contemporarily, five million Palestinians living under occupation in the West Bank and Gaza), we can be distant, almost unmoved. But when we bring the stories of "one" into our immediate circle, we can then begin to understand the magnitude of the trauma when we multiply these single stories exponentially.

Lastly, for "many-to-one" thinking to translate into actions, we need to do more than empathize, but rather include the Other's experiences into our own: to own them and to respond to them as we would want others to respond to our traumas, and see their interests as connected to our personal and tribal interests. It is important to understand why these transformations are so rare. Humanizing the Other is antithetical to tribal thinking. We need to be precise in how we talk about this.

Many people engage in interfaith or intercultural exchanges. Many people recognize that learning about someone else broadens our horizons and can lead to greater harmony in the world. However, traversing the invisible (but nevertheless complex and deeply entrenched) barrier between competing narratives is a very different matter.

In short, we each have to give something up. A Palestinian asking a Jew about how the Holocaust has affected them, or a Jew asking a Palestinian about how Israel impacts their life, requires being invested in the answer, even if the answer runs counter to one's personal or tribal interests.

Being willing to divest even a small part of your personal and tribal interests is no small feat. Personal and tribal interests are oxygen for the fire of conflict. Personal and tribal interests are entirely based on a zero-sum paradigm: I win, you lose/you win, I lose. Moving towards shared interests necessitates a willingness from both parties to move away from the zero-sum paradigm.

Michael Dan's *The Two-State Dilemma: A Game Theory Perspective on the Israeli-Palestinian Conflict* offers an alternative to the zero-sum way of viewing the conflict. In short, Dan's optimal solution is arrived at through the "Prisoner's Dilemma," which requires both sides to trust the other and take greater risk but receive a much greater reward. In other words, each side may want to have it all, but this risks both sides losing everything. In Dan's game theory model, the "pot" of what we can gain is much greater if we cooperate than if we don't.

Dan's book is focused on the struggle itself while we are focused on the struggle within the two Diasporas. What is actually at risk for us over here is much less than for those over there, but the trifecta of identity, trauma, and victimhood obscures this fact. We fight with each other over ideas as if our survival depends on it. Beginning with a desire to include the Other in our frame of reference is an essential first step in pushing back on the zero-sum nature of our discourse.

As we have outlined in Chapter 4, the tragedy of the Holocaust for Jews, which led in part to the creation of the State of Israel, resulted in another tragedy for Palestinians: the Nakba. These compounding tragedies are mourned separately. When we personalize each other's trauma, we create spaces where justice for one cannot be achieved by inflicting injustice on the Other, where their tragedy is interwoven with our own. When we see each other as individuals, "otherizing" becomes much more difficult. The media noise about the struggle, from both sides, intentionally entrenches the notion that the Other is so unlike us that they are unknowable. It is up to us, individually, to counteract this way of thinking.

SEPARATING THE PAST FROM THE PRESENT

Seeing the Other individually is vital to dismantling the wall, but we also need to create distance between the past and the present so we can envision a future based on a reimagined present, one that is separate from the past. Imagine a curtain between the past and the present, and that what has happened is separate from what is happening now.

In the Israel-Palestine discussion in the Diasporas, there is a pronounced difference between how baby boomers, Gen Xers, millennials, and Gen Zs think. Baby boomers are deeply engaged in stories of the Holocaust (and the memories of the 1967 and 1973 wars) or the Nakba (and the consequences of the 1967 and 1973 wars on Palestinians), Gen Xers less so, and millennials and Gen Zs even less. In short, younger Jews and Palestinians, by and large, don't get why their parents and grandparents focus so much on the past. Many young Jews find pro-Israel arguments that are rooted in past traumas to be outdated and unhelpful. This also applies to many young Palestinians who are calling for a democratic state with equal rights for all the people who today live in historic Palestine, rather than the elimination of the settler-Jewish presence the way their parents did.

Though to varying degrees, all of us fall into the trap of conflating what once happened with what is happening today, baby boomers are far more likely to succumb to this way of thinking, especially where Israel-Palestine is concerned. Younger generations have been much more able to separate past traumas from present occurrences.[76] This is not to say that they are immune from the trauma-inducing rhetoric, from both sides, meant to inflame feelings of perpetual victimhood. The past, particularly in terms of trauma, is being operationalized, using fear as a means of keeping us in our camps and ensuring our loyalty to the cause.

For many Jews, thinking outside of their tragic past is just too much to deal with. The scope of the Holocaust is incomprehensible (and not just for Jews). This is difficult terrain, and it matters. In psychotherapy, a variety of tools are used to help a person distinguish what has happened from what is happening. This type of therapy guides us through a transformative process where we can be released from the emotional prison created by painful events in our past. The events are no less real, but they are contained in a manner that they no longer rule our present or predict our future.

How does one ask Jews to do this in terms of the Holocaust? Is it heresy to even suggest that the Holocaust needs to play a smaller role in the Jewish narrative?

While no amount of apologies or reparations can fully address the horrors of the Holocaust, there has been (and continues to be) global recognition of the antisemitism that led to the Holocaust and of the failure of most of the Western world to respond to the horror that unfolded in Europe.

The ultimate goal in individual trauma therapy is repair—healing—and we do need to heal from the past. As many younger Jews are already doing, we need to be able to compartmentalize, even when it comes to such an overwhelming tragedy as the Holocaust.

This can only be done by intentionally separating today's antisemitism from that of Nazi Germany. A swastika on a Jewish gravestone, often spray-painted by a white supremacist or other disaffected person, while an affront to all that is decent, does not hold the power of a swastika on the armband of an SS commander. Even the phrase "Free Palestine, from the river to the sea" can be viewed not as a call for another "final solution" but as a call for freedom.

On the face of it, in spite of ongoing antisemitism, Jews enjoy prominent status in Western societies. But, with what we know about identity, trauma, and victimhood, this logic is not enough. The separation of the past does not occur through magical thinking, but by seeing that the circumstances on the ground have drastically changed. We can learn to see an antisemitic comment or incident in isolation, rather than as proof of the past replaying over again. This is part of the repair process, and we need to intentionally do the emotional work of making these separations.

For Palestinians, this separation is understandably more challenging, as the shockwaves of 1948 continue to reverberate throughout their daily lives: the Occupation, the Gaza blockade, land confiscations, creeping annexation—and the myriad other injustices they suffer. And as long as there is no real recognition of the injustice of the Nakba, from both Israel or the Western powers, it seems incomprehensible that the past can be separated from the present. This doesn't mean that every Israeli action is a replay of 1948, but asking Palestinians to make this distinction, under the current conditions, is unreasonable.

There are many wonderful examples of Palestinians and Jews in Israel/Palestine who have refused to see every incident, no matter how egregious, as proof that the struggle is permanently entrenched. Instead they have focused on coming together and supporting each other with a vision of a peaceful future together.

In short, seeing the past in every action and reaction in the present will determine whether the conflict will continue. If images of Palestinians protesting the Occupation (with words or with violence) prompts a traumatic reaction, bringing up memories of historical attacks on Jews, how can Jews move forward? Or, if Holocaust remembrance ceremonies are seen simply as a distraction from stealing of Palestinian land, how can Palestinians move forward? We need to intentionally separate what has happened from what is happening. If we begin to sever past wounds from present events, this way of thinking will recalibrate how we work together today and predict a whole new way of interrelating in the future.

We must "re-member" our group to include the Other and the Other's suffering, hopes, and future possibilities.

REJECTING GROUPTHINK

We have outlined two essential steps towards the Other in dismantling the wall. The first is what we call moving from "many to one," shifting from seeing the Other as a monolith to seeing them as a collection of individual narratives and experiences. The second is creating a separation between the past and the present so that the future can be based primarily on what is happening now, rather than being locked in the prison of a past reality. The third step involves looking for knowledge outside of our tribes.

An alternate title for this book might be "Rejecting Groupthink." Groupthink is a label that many social psychologists use to define the phenomenon of social pressure that can lead to less-than-optimal decision-making within groups. These groups tend to have a cohesive social identity that bonds them together. As we have laid out, in the Israel-Palestine discourse, the bonds of social identity have been cemented by our collective memories of historical trauma and victimhood narratives (ITV). We caution here that groupthink is an important variable, but not the whole picture. While most of us are affected by external pressures, this does not absolve us of personal responsibility, nor do we suggest that our readers are brainwashed automatons that are unable to make sound decisions. The case we have made is that the toxic mix of a strong ITV and well-oiled propaganda machines has distorted our view of the Other and of the struggle as a whole.

While one might reasonably conclude that the antithesis of groupthink is thinking for oneself, it isn't quite as straightforward as that. Groupthink, or tribal thinking, amalgamates our individual identities and experiences, thereby intensifying our confidence in the reliability of our conclusions. The pathway from groupthink starts not by being more individualistic, but by widening one's group. Referring back to Edward Markham's notion of "widening the circle," to break away from groupthink we must expose ourselves to contrary knowledge and experiences. Palestinians and Jews who have learned from each other are no less Palestinian or less Jewish as a result of their collaboration, but over time they can form a "shared identity." Their decision making comes from hearing each other's narratives. Groupthink is a narrowing of the circle, a contraction of possibilities. Values-forward thinking must include the narrative of the Other. Justice-centered decision-making requires us to expand our listening and then act out of this new learning, despite tribal pressures to conform.

A final key aspect of rejecting groupthink is to recognize that none of us is blessed with a permanent wide-angle lens; we all, to one degree or another, are prone to tunnel vision. In a car, there is a warning in the side-view mirrors that says, "Objects may be closer than they appear." Similarly, our perspective should come with a warning that says, "Our view of the Other may be tainted by our tribal instincts." Most importantly, we need to view the Other as a resource—a remedy for our tainted thinking.

This encounter with the Other is not entered into lightly. Our interest in the Other must come from a place of needing to understand something outside of our current perspective. It should not be an encounter with someone who is unwilling to widen their circle, but rather a shared action, done to broaden our circle of understanding and enable us to partner with those who have been outside of our communal fold.

Each of the pathways we have outlined in this chapter pulls us away from our tribally-driven identity, trauma, and victimhood. These pathways towards values-forward thinking can be useful ways to construct a genuinely new view of the Other. Yet these are not simple remedies. Our tribalized thinking functions habitually, limiting our worldview, toxifying our discourse, and trapping us in an endless cycle of whataboutism. The larger shift we must make is to work in spaces where the narratives collide. Our final chapter lays out a road map for doing this work—to sit with discomfort, to press forward, to resist the noise and create a new narrative that is inclusive of the views of the Other.

CHAPTER 10
WORKING IN SPACES WHERE THE NARRATIVES COLLIDE

"We don't need a peace agreement to live in peace."
—Osama Elawat (Webinar, The Parents Circle, March 31, 2021)

Is the move from tribal, trauma-driven, inward protectionism to values-forward thinking an abstract concept for you, or is it the seismic shift we think it is? The answer lies in our willingness to work at the "collision points" where the narratives seem incompatible.

In Part II, we looked at three of these collision points: antisemitism, Zionism and the Nakba, and Palestinian resistance. We need to be clear about where these fundamental clashes of tribal experiences come from and how to intentionally challenge our resistance to the Other's narrative.

ANTISEMITISM
In Chapter 4, we summarized the antithetical feelings of Jews and Palestinians about antisemitism:

> To a Jew, antisemitism is a past trauma, a present trauma and an almost-guaranteed future trauma. Antisemitism is a thread that runs through the tapestry of Jewish life. It

is ever-present, foreboding, and certain. It weaves its way, often surreptitiously and silently through even the happiest of times. It is the monster whose haunting presence breathes down one's neck, refusing to allow any Jew to forget its existence.

To a Palestinian, antisemitism is a muzzle, a weapon to silence, defend, and deflect from or otherwise discredit critics of Israel's actions. It is a club to clobber the heads of those taking a stand for Palestine, and the shackle that ties down the hands of solidarity. It is the boot that presses down one's neck, choking speech, silencing thought, removing voice, and eliminating hope. It's an "occupation" of the narrative.

How do we look at these statements from a values perspective rather than from tribal positions borne out of our identity, trauma, and victimhood? In practical terms, it begins by living in the paradigms we presented in the last chapter: seeing the individual first; not how do Jews or Palestinians feel, but how does the Jew or the Palestinian in front of us feel? Step two, realize that past pain is influencing our (and the Other's) present reaction. Lastly, consciously choosing to see the Other's view as separate from our need to support and protect our tribe and our tribe's position.

How might these apply to some of the cases we laid out in the chapter on antisemitism? For example, the firestorm created by Rep. Ilhan Omar when she stated, "It's all about the Benjamins." The reaction to this and other statements she made positioned her as a stereotypical representation of all Muslims (or leftists). She was not seen as an individual but as a representation of the universal threat posed to Jews by all critics of Israel (and presumed antisemites). We saw people we know and respect respond on a purely traumatic level, drawing direct links to medieval blood libels and Omar's statements, seemingly inferring that her statements are a present risk to Jewish safety were and unable to think outside of their tribal belonging.

While her words were clearly imperfect, Omar was shining a light on how the pro-Israel lobby used its fundraising and political clout to silence Palestinian resistance. If we can reposition this as a call for universal human rights and not be distracted by our loyalty to tribe and historical trauma and instead be values-focused, we could engage in the transformative work necessary to both listen differently and respond actively to the Other's plight. Sadly, the vociferous reaction to Omar's statements did more to prove her point than to dissuade her and others from pushing back on Israeli policy.

Demolishing the wall requires us to see each and every reaction with a degree of nuance. When a Jew says they are feeling the sting of antisemitism, the pain is real. When a Palestinian, or a supporter of the Palestinian cause, suggests that antisemitism is being weaponized in order to further oppress them, it is also real. For many Jews, the reality and power of antisemitism is so unquestionable that positioning it as a weapon to silence is itself a further example of antisemitism. For a Palestinian, the chant of "antisemitism, antisemitism, antisemitism" overwhelms their ability (or interest) to see the pain behind it. We have been mired in an unsolvable back and forth of what is and isn't antisemitism. Antisemitism is real, and so is its weaponization to silence criticism. These truths can and must exist together. Most importantly, values-forward thinking requires us to care about them together and not allow one to overwhelm the other.

Applying the three paradigms from Chapter 9 to the discourse around antisemitism means thinking outside of our tribal silos. The impact of antisemitism needs to be seen, first, at the micro (individual) level before we deal with the macro (group). We need to interrupt the past-present link—"It did happen, so it must be happening now and it will happen again." Finally, we must push back on groupthink, which in reality is not thinking at all, but an emotional reaction. The antisemitism argument needs to be reformed as it has trapped Jews, Palestinians, and much of the Western world in an endless blame game that allows a status quo where the suffering of Palestinians in the Occupied Territories goes on unabated, ensuring that the struggle will go on indefinitely.

ZIONISM AND THE NAKBA

Jews and Palestinians' core resistance to each other and each other's narrative lies in how each thinks about and/or discounts Zionism and the Nakba. The irreconcilable reality that freedom for one came at the expense of another is behind much of the handwringing of peace-minded individuals on both sides. The Israeli-Palestinian struggle has become the poster child for intractability. From the narrative perspective, there is little common ground or even reason to hope that a solution can be found. The pro-Israel lobby has tried unrelentingly to insist that the Zionist project was always, and still is, an ideal mixture of the fulfilling of the promise of self-determination for Jews on their ancestral homeland and a democratic state for all—if only the Arabs had gone along with the plan. Similarly, many Palestinians argue that the Jewish plan was only to colonize their land and ethnically cleanse their people. We hope that our readers have concluded that neither of these arguments tells the whole truth.

But our book is not about "absolute truth," but rather on working through contradictions in the narratives.

So what are the core contradictions in the narratives of Zionism and the Nakba?

1. Zionism is the realization of a Jewish homeland. Zionism is the destruction of Palestinian society.

2. Eretz Israel is the ancestral homeland of the Jewish people and their God-given right. Arab Palestinians have been the dominant presence in the land since the seventh century.

3. The Arab states' rejection of the UN partition plan in 1947 and Arab hostility toward Israel were the prime causes of the 1948 war (and this pattern of Arab rejectionism was true in all subsequent wars). The UN partition plan was grossly unfair, no one would have accepted it, and the Arab states were just coming to the aid of their fellow Palestinian Arabs. Furthermore, blaming Arabs for all the conflicts is classic scapegoating, as Israel is the primary military power in the region with the backing of the US, the world's most powerful military.

4. Arabs massacred Jews too, and most Palestinian Arabs fled Palestine on their own accord. Zionist forces were responsible for many massacres and carried out planned and intentional ethnic cleansing of Palestinians.

5. At least 800,000 Jews were expelled from Arab countries in the decades following the creation of Israel, while 750,000 Palestinians became refugees in surrounding countries in 1948, creating a humanitarian and existential catastrophe for Palestinians.

6. Israel has the right to secure borders and self-defense, and Hamas is primarily responsible for any and all the violence that occurs. After fifty-plus years of occupation, the Gaza blockade and settlement expansion are in violation of international law and continue to inflict countless suffering on Palestinians.

It is easy to see how identity, trauma, and victimhood play out here. Whatever pain you think you suffered, ours is worse. And the race to the bottom continues. How then can values-forward thinking propel us out of these tribal trenches?

The first two contradictory narratives relate to the struggle between Israel's existence and the cost of that existence to another: Jewish safety and self-determination coming at the price of Palestinian society, and Israel being the Jews' ancestral homeland, versus Palestinian Arabs having been the majority presence for over 1,400 years. These arguments sit at the crux of the struggle. The first is a self-preservation claim: Israel is a necessity, due largely to the Holocaust, and while Palestinians had nothing to do with the Holocaust, they have paid the price for Jewish safety from it. In the second case, the Jewish narrative is driven primarily by religious and historical claims.

To our Jewish (or those who are generally pro-Israel) readers, don't give up on us yet. Let's put values-forward thinking to work. Of course, to differing degrees, both peoples have legitimate claims to the land, and Zionism is partly an answer to centuries of oppression suffered by Jews. Yet, from a justice and values perspective, we have to deal with the central problem with Zionism: freedom for one comes at the cost of another, and that, morally, Palestinians have a much stronger claim to the land than do Jews. It is most natural for Jews to resist this, but if we look at Israel-Palestine through a justice lens, as was said in the film *Colliding Dreams*, "the bride was already engaged."

In our discourse, this means pushing past the trauma-driven reaction to such statements and going deeper. For Jews, it means confronting the painful reality that Zionism, as a project, took from one to give to another. For Palestinians, it means not setting aside the fact that Jewish history has necessitated the need for security, despite the fact that Palestinians have paid the price for that security.

Dealing with the reality that freedom for one came at the cost of another is at the heart of the struggle in the discourse here in the West. If you wrestle with the question of whether or not Jewish safety has come at too great a cost to Palestinians, then you may have to come face-to-face with the reality that the Zionist project itself could be seriously flawed. This is not an easy pill to swallow.

There is no magic reset button. We need to find a way to confront the reality of Zionism as the cause for the Nakba, while working to find a just way for sharing the land going forward.

The next two contradictory narratives get at who is to blame and how much responsibility each should take on. First, the UN partition plan and the overarching narrative of who is to blame for 1948 and the ensuing conflicts. The second, Arab reprisal attacks on Jews and the eviction of Jews from Arab lands versus the cleansing of Palestinians from the land, through massacres, fear, and intentional ethnic cleansing. Neither of these is a simple choice of one or the other, but there are important guideposts that can help us move outside of our tribal positions. As we have already brought out, the claim that Arab Palestinians should have acquiesced to an agreement that they saw as grossly unfair is a form of blaming the victim for not accepting their victimization.

Similarly, the extent to which the removal of Palestinian Arabs was pre-planned has been debated since 1948. We need to complicate simplistic analyses, that Arab Palestinians were expelled (and massacred) or fled out of fear (or, in some cases, because Arab leaders told them that they would be able to return soon). What is irrefutable is that Jewish leadership knew, as early as the dawn of the twentieth century, that for the project of Zionism to succeed, Palestinian Arabs would have to be moved out of the land, at least to some extent. What we are left to deal with, from a justice perspective, is that even if we accept that the Arab countries' intervention was a contributing factor and that some Palestinians fled voluntarily, there is no getting around the reality that at least 750,000 people fled or were expelled and, to this day, have never been allowed to return.

The next contradictory narrative deals with justification. Because one has suffered, does that justify inflicting suffering on another? Is the frequent response to the expulsion of Palestinians in 1948, that Jews were also evicted from Arab lands and in similar numbers, a reasonable justification? First, the justifications for the massacres and expulsions in 1948 (Arabs rejected the UN partition plan, Arab states attacked Israel, Arabs also committed massacres, and "War is terrible and bad things happen") must be critically examined, as we have attempted to do in this book, through a justice lens. This perspective pushes beyond ideas of one trauma justifying another and safety for one being achieved on the backs of another. From a values and justice viewpoint, we need to see the Jewish desire to return to their biblical homeland as important, but not as a justification for displacing those who were already there. Second, as we discussed in Chapter 5, the connection of 1948 and Jews leaving Arab lands, either by choice or by necessity, is not wholly reasonable. Again, from a trauma perspective, there is no doubt that Jews who fled Arab countries in the 1950s and '60s deserve our empathy. We personally know families who have been deeply affected by these experiences, and they do matter. However, trying to compare the two is not productive. We need to recognize that the backlash towards Jews in Arab countries was a direct result of the 1948 war and the loss of Palestine. Most of the Jews who fled went to Israel (often because Israel encouraged them to come) or to other welcoming places, rather than becoming refugees, living often in unwelcome places and in squalid conditions. Palestinians are not responsible for the actions taken by the Arab countries. It is always important to acknowledge trauma, but never to misrepresent or excuse the trauma we have caused to another.

Finally, the endless back-and-forth on whether or not security concerns justify the inflicting of such hardships on Palestinians is a true zero-sum argument. The "Israel has a right to security" stance assumes that the only reasonable response to Hamas and other resistance forces is repression. It precludes the idea that there are Israeli violations that require resistance and that ending these violations is the most just response. This argument also ignores the right of safety and security for Palestinians.

As we move to the last facet of how we must retell the colliding narratives, Palestinian resistance, we need to stop equivocating resistance with terrorism, and peaceful protest movements with antisemitism.

We need to recall our three paradigms: seeing the Other as an individual rather than a monolith, drawing the curtain between what once happened and what is happening, and thinking outside of our tribal bubble. These can provide us with an anchor to rely on when the sea gets rough. Each of these counternarratives stirs up deep emotions for many of us, but in order to resist the default position of identity, trauma, and victimhood, we need to be able to have these guideposts to help us avoid retreating into our historical traumas.

PALESTINIAN RESISTANCE

Perhaps the most intractable aspect of the current discourse over here is the so-called resistance to the resistance. The fault line in the discourse in North America is largely framed around the debate between Palestinian resistance and counterclaims of antisemitism. This plays out online, in political debates, on college and university campuses, and in society as a whole. We have done a deep dive into this discussion in several chapters of this book. To begin to break out of this endless back-and-forth, we offer three concrete shifts in how we talk about Israel-Palestine in the West:

1. The Israeli-Palestinian struggle and antisemitism need to be viewed as separate entities. This means that claims that

criticism of Israel is a threat to self-determination (and therefore Jewish survival) need to be viewed through a new lens, one that recognizes that resistance to a military occupation will, by necessity, include resistance to the occupying state, not to the right to self-determination or the right of Jews to be defined as a people.

2. Current delineations about what is and isn't antisemitism are inadequate and need to work from a default position that asserting antisemitism as a means of silencing uncomfortable discourses about Palestinian experiences of oppression is never acceptable.

3. Jews need to appreciate that Palestinian resistance is inseparable from Palestinian identity—that to exist is to resist. Palestinians, for their part, need to be able to separate legitimate concerns of antisemitism from ones only designed to silence them.

The first two points work in tandem and are perhaps the most challenging for Jews. Since the creation of the IHRA definition, there have been at least two new attempts to offer a more nuanced stance on the connection between criticism of Israel and antisemitism: the Nexus definition[77] and the Jerusalem Declaration on Antisemitism.[78] In both cases, the drafters intentionally draw a clearer line between criticizing Israel and antisemitism than does the IHRA definition. But making this connection, even from the standpoint of pushing back on the weaponization of antisemitism, keeps alive the notion that there is an inherent connection. Conflating the two keeps open the possibility of delegitimizing any criticism.

Returning to the idea of the two metanarratives—the Holocaust and the Nakba—criticism of Israel, particularly criticism that questions the legitimacy of the Zionist project, from a trauma perspective, recalls the wounds of the Shoah. (Israel, symbolically, was the redemption of the Jews from the Shoah; threatening Israel is therefore threatening a recurrence of the Holocaust.) Similarly, using antisemitism as a way of silencing criticism is, again from a trauma perspective, silencing the pain of the Nakba for Palestinians. We must take these links seriously, but not equivocate the two.

Even the harshest critiques of Israel, including calling it an apartheid state or a settler-colonial enterprise, are not in themselves antisemitic. This is an extremely important distinction. And we need to recognize the tremendous resentment making this connection enlivens in Palestinians.

We, of course, acknowledge that, particularly in Europe, some antisemitic attacks were carried out by Islamist extremists who hold deep hostility toward Israel and lump all Jews into the same bucket (along with the Israeli military and the Israeli government). The key is to delineate between these relatively rare cases and the reality that "physical" antisemitic attacks in North America are usually perpetrated by far-right, neo-fascists. Additionally, as we focus here on values, the more attention we pay to the root causes of Palestinian resistance in all its forms, rather than working to silence that resistance, the better chance we have at creating a justice-centered discourse.

The third shift that is required is for us to understand Palestinian resistance in a similar way that most of us in the West—Jews and non-Jews—have come to reject antisemitism: as an existential necessity. As we have charted, for most Palestinians, to resist is to exist. The status quo in the North American discourse on Israel-Palestine is to only view Palestinian resistance in relation to how it threatens Israel. In any discussion of the Other, it is imperative that we flip our vantage point to see what they are seeing, outside of how it affects us. If we accept that resisting antisemitism is a "Western value," why do we not also see Palestinian resistance to occupation in a similar light?

Resistance to oppression is a Western value. The problem has been that Palestinians, and therefore their acts of resistance, are seen as the Other, outside of our Western consciousness. We have outlined several causes for this, but it is time to "widen the circle." If, as we contend, othering happens as a result of placing someone outside of our circle of belonging, then we can reverse course. The justice moment we have re-ferred to throughout this book is knocking on our collective conscience.

The us/them paradigm in regard to Jews and Palestinians (and even Israel and Palestine) will only ensure that the debate remains entirely polarized and that no real action will be taken.

Here are the transformative questions:
1. Will you widen your circle to include the Other and the Other's narrative?
2. Will you include the trauma of the Other in your view of the struggle?
3. Will you push back on those who want to keep us in our tribal silos?
4. Will you embrace a justice-centered discourse and reject the discourse driven by us/them thinking and historical trauma?
5. Can you see yourself and others as individuals rather than collectives?
6. Can you break the cycle of everlasting victimhood?
7. Can we work together as Palestinians/Jews/allies in the West to make these wall-shattering changes happen?

AFTERWORD

Throughout this book, as co-authors, we have spoken as one voice to Jews, to Palestinians, and to the many interested parties. We would like to now speak directly to our communities. While maintaining some distance from our personal stories and natural tribal belongings was necessary for us, we recognize that this was not wholly possible. We trust that our readers who do not identify as Jewish or Palestinian will also benefit from our speaking directly to our respective groups.

JEFF - BEING JEWISH MEANS MANY THINGS

For me, being Jewish is both a belonging and a loss of belonging. I cherish the holidays, the study of Torah with other Jews, and the shared language of customs and food. Most of all, I cherish the Jewish values of *tzedakah* (charity) and *tikkun olam* (to heal the world). I also value our history, which includes the painful remembering of our traumatic existence.

I'm troubled that we have stayed in our victimhood far too long. Our fears have been preventing us from appreciating and fully embracing the free and inclusive world that the vast majority of us have the privilege of living in. My journey out of victimhood, in large part, has come from including the Palestinian story in my story.

An important part of overcoming our historical victimhood is confronting the cost of our current freedom (Zionism) to Palestinians—to share our painful pasts and be part of reconstructing

139

the future. There are groups that inspire me in Israel-Palestine, who have reached beyond their own victimhood stories, such as The Parents Circle-Families Forum and Combatants for Peace. By including the trauma of another in our story, we become less self-protective and more justice oriented.

As we have explored in this book, the synthesizing of Jewish identity and Zionism has blurred the cultural with the political and religious identity with religious nationalism, keeping us isolated from the narrative of the Palestinians, a narrative in which we have played, and continue to play, a significant part.

I have had to ask myself if being a Zionist and being Jewish are inseparable. If I reject Israel as an ethnocentric democracy, do I have to hand over my Jewish "membership card"? Am I less of a Jew by being deeply engaged in Palestinian human rights? These questions then morph into other questions. Do I believe in Jewish self-determination? Do I then define this as a commitment to a Jewish state rather than simply the right to be a people?

Finally, and most significantly, am I a Zionist? For me, this is the wrong question. Zionism, and more importantly, my (or any other Jew's) views on it, is the wrong measuring stick. Our identity as Jews must be untethered from our views on Israel. We have come to believe that what bonds us is Eretz Israel—the land of and for the Jews. To me, what has bound us together are our heritage, our culture, and to varying degrees, our religious practice and our core values.

Israel is a physical place, but it has been made into much more. It has become the flashpoint at which our loyalties are tested. To be Jewish is to support Israel. This needs to be complicated. It assumes a naive retelling of history that the effects on Palestinians were largely unintentional. We, as Jews, need to come face-to-face with the reality that the expulsion of Palestinians was a necessary and intentional action for creating a Jewish-majority state—we chose to displace a people so that we could take their place. If we face this, we can no longer see supporting Israel in the simplistic way that we do.

In looking at how to repair this, I care less about one-state, two-state, confederation, or any other long-term resolution; rather my concern is centered on how we redress the injustices that the creation of the State of Israel has created. The mantra of Jewish safety must be considered within the framework of justice for Palestinians, remembering that the greatest threat to Jewish security is our failure to create a lasting peace with Palestinians.

Our discourse about the Israeli-Palestinian struggle usually boils down to arguments over who is the greatest victim. This pattern must be broken. This victim approach has taught our children to be afraid. Is speaking to a Palestinian supporter of BDS a dangerous undertaking? Do we not want our children to be curious and find points of agreement with those from different backgrounds and experiences?

I challenge each of us to broaden how we define our Jewishness and to do the hard work of dealing with the consequences of Zionism to Palestinians. This is tough work, but we have done it before, and we can do it again. Throughout Jewish history, we have had to reevaluate and adjust. It is time to apply this to Israel by valuing and addressing not just Jewish concerns, but Palestinian rights.

To include the Other has always been the Jewish way, and we need to honor this historic commitment in Israel-Palestine, Palestine-Israel.

RAJA - FROM THE RIVER TO THE SEA

What is Palestine?

We know what Palestine was before 1948, but what is it today? A cause for freedom, certainly, but what else? Having lost the land, what is it that we continue to hold on to, beyond the memories?

It turns out the idea of Palestine is bigger than the land itself. The idea of a people who hold on to their Palestinian roots despite being physically uprooted is the challenge that we Palestinians have taken on; from Chile to China, Alaska to Angola, wherever you find us, the roots are safely tucked away with us. We pass them on from one generation to the next, faithfully, deliberately, defiantly, so that Palestine, the idea, does not die.

We have become a stubborn people. We had to. With fortitude came stubbornness. Though we've come to a point that it has become difficult for us to change, to move forward. So, we hold on to more than our roots, to some ossified, rejectionist attitudes.

We are stuck in 1948. I get it. Most Jews (and the West) have never acknowledged 1948 as the deliberate Nakba (catastrophe) that it was. While Jewish trauma of the Holocaust has been fully recognized (in film, theater, literature, legislation, compensation), our trauma, the Nakba, remains largely obscured. I know the temptation is for us to stay in 1948 until our Nakba has been redressed.

We are an angry people. For good reason. But at times we project our anger in ways that are self-defeating. We take to insulting the Jews, attacking their peoplehood, and voicing doubts about the extent of the Holocaust. How does any of this help? Accepting that antisemitism exists and that horrors have been inflicted on the Jewish people does not take away from our cause.

Our people have been wronged so many times by history (by Europeans, Zionists, Americans, other Arabs) that we have become skeptical and suspicious. So suspicious that we often don't trust each other, are not able to work together, and are intolerant towards ideas different from our own. Outliers appear to us as sell-outs because they dare stray from the pack.

In this book we've talked about how antisemitism has been weaponized to silence and even marginalize us. It's frustrating, deceitful, and hurtful, but it should not dissuade us from understanding how Jews feel and why. They too have traumas that have stayed with them to this day, just as ours have. If we expect them to understand our traumas, we should aim to understand theirs. There's no other way.

I must admit I wince every time I hear the word "Israel." As long as Israel continues to embody the negation and erasure of my past, I cannot wish for her a future that enjoys peace and security. There can be no peace within us until the crimes and atrocities of 1948 have been atoned for. Until the prime minister of Israel says to us, without obfuscation, "On behalf of the Jews of Israel, I am sorry for having taken everything from you. Please forgive us."

I understand our anger at the wrongs that have been inflicted on us unabated for over a century. I can understand Palestinian frustration with a world order where the injustices continue to accumulate by sheer right of might. I understand the indignity Palestinians feel when their rights are outweighed by the rights of others, where Israel's "right to defend itself" and the Jewish insatiable appetite for security are not reciprocated to fellow humans of the Palestinian extraction.

I also understand that, as long as we continue to feel, think, and act as victims, we will continue to be victimized. I'm delighted by the rise of Palestinian leadership in North America that has embraced the struggle of other racialized and marginalized communities and called for the universality of rights for all—Black, Indigenous, women, people of color, LGBTQ+, Palestinians. This leadership's vision for a "one-person-one-vote" democracy (or some other form of binational/confederated statehood) in all of historic Palestine embraces the Jews of Israel as fellow co-inhabitants of a future Israel-Palestine/Palestine-Israel. That's a vision of a shared future I can get behind. I can imagine no other just solution.

Let us get on that road to peace with justice.

ACKNOWLEDGEMENTS

As in any large undertaking, this book would be impossible without support from many people. This has come in the form of encouragement, reading various iterations of the book, providing invaluable feedback, and connecting us with other wise and helpful people. For this, among others, we thank Mohammed Alhroub, Jehad Aliweiwi, Cheri Gurse, Greg Khalil, Noah and Sandra Mintz, Dr. Karen Mock, Judith Ramirez, Ken Stern, Sarah Sturm, Ronit Yarosky, Ann Wilkinson, Raymond Young, and Noura Zaina.

Many, many thanks to those who lent us their brainstorming and expertise, including Peter Beinart, Neil Caplan, Dana Dajani, Khalid Elgindy, Natalie Fingerhut, Lisa Goldman, Paul Golob, Jasmin Habib, Walker Robbins, and Josh Ruebner.

With love and gratitude, we thank valued friends and family for their support, mentorship, technical advice, and a beautiful writing retreat, including Jehad Aliweiwi, Judith Ramirez, Lyn and Duncan Turnbull, Ann Wilkinson, and Emilie Wilkinson.

And finally, a special thank-you to our editor and the wonderful people at Interlink Publishing, who made our book a reality.

ENDNOTES

1 "What is Israel's Separation Wall in the West Bank?," Palestine Remix, https://interactive.aljazeera.com/aje/palestineremix/wall.html, retrieved February 21, 2023.

2 Daniel Pomerantz, "Why Did Israel Really Build a Security Barrier?," HonestReporting (2018), https://www.youtube.com/watch?v=xP28QVfrRfw.

3 In May of 2021, after several inflammatory actions, including Israeli soldiers raiding Al-Aqsa Mosque, threatened evictions of Palestinians from their homes in the Sheikh Jarrah neighborhood of East Jerusalem, and riots fomented by far-right Jewish groups in mixed towns, Hamas sent rockets into Israel and Israel responded with intense bombing in Gaza. This initiated a new global response that has begun to shift the discourse in the West about Israel-Palestine.

4 *The Holocaust and the Nakba: A New Grammar of Trauma and History*, editors B. Bashir and A. Goldberg, Columbia University Press, 2018.

5 Haidt, J. and Lukianoff, G. (2018). *The Coddling of the American Mind: How Good Intentions and Bad Ideas Are Setting Up a Generation for Failure*. New York: Penguin Press.

6 Malcolm Hoenlein, "There is no Hebrew word for history," Israel National News, May 29, 2017, http://www.israelnationalnews.com/Articles/Article.aspx/20565. Spoken at a rally in 2017 for "Jerusalem Day." British labor minister David Miliband made a similar quote: "I

do not speak Hebrew, but I understand there is no word for 'history.'" The closest word for it is 'memory.'"

7   We may think of "facts" and "truths" interchangeably, but they are distinct from each other. A fact is immutable—drop something and it falls. Truth instead can be viewed personally. "My truth" is often infused with beliefs and values that separate it from "pure" fact.

8   On April 9, 1948, 130 commandos of the Irgun and the Stern Gang attacked the Arab village of Deir Yassin (*Remembering Deir Yassin: The Future of Israel and Palestine* (Olive Branch Press, 1998). Several sources, including McGowan, place the number of Palestinians killed at about 100. Other sources estimate the death toll as high as 250. *The New York Times* reported the final count at 254 on April 13, 1948 (http://www.deiryassin.org/mas.html). Charles Smith's book *Palestine and the Arab-Israeli Conflict* also states that "the bodies of men, women and children were mutilated and stuffed down wells" (Smith, 1992). Counternarratives about the massacre, like *The Birth of a Palestinian Nation: The Myth of the Deir Yassin Massacre* (Milstein, 2012), have also been written, calling it "the massacre that didn't happen." However, many stories from Israeli soldiers who were there, including members of the organization Breaking the Silence confirm many of the details referenced here.

9   The term "anti-Semitism" was first coined in 1879 by a German, Wilhelm Marr, to refer to political campaigns against Jews, viewing them as both a race and a religion. The spelling of the word is contested. It is typically spelled "anti-Semitism," but some scholars argue that this misses the original intent, describing feelings and actions against Jews, not all "Semites," which includes Arabs (https://holocaustremembrance.sharepoint.com/.../download.aspx). This newer word, "antisemitism," refers to beliefs and actions targeting Jews, not all Semites.

10   Zur, O., "Psychology of Victimhood: Don't Blame the Victim." *Journal of Couple and Relational Therapy*, January 2008.

11   Gerard Baker, "The Rise of Woke Anti-Semitism," *The Wall Street Journal* (May 24, 2021), https://www.wsj.com/articles/

the-rise-of-woke-anti-semitism-11621881999. The sentiment of antisemitism being the "oldest form of hatred" is often used to frame antisemitism as unique from all other forms of prejudice, particularly during times of intense criticism directed at Israel, as in the Gaza War of May 2021.

12 While we look more fully at this in Chapter 5, this 78 percent figure is often contested by pro-Israel groups, suggesting that Transjordan is part of Palestine and therefore much less than 78 percent of the land was taken by the Jews. While Transjordan was part of the British Mandate for Palestine, the name Transjordan always referred to the lands east of the Jordan River.

13 https://www.dw.com/en/german-parliament-condemns-anti-semitic-bds-movement/a-48779516

14 Aaron Reich, "Ilhan Omar voted 2019's antisemite of the year," *The Jerusalem Post* (January 7, 2020) https://www.jpost.com/diaspora/antisemitism/ilhan-omar-voted-2019s-antisemite-of-the-year-613308

15 Emanuel Miller & Shoshanna Keats Jasloll, "How to Criticize Israel Without being Antisemitic," Backspin, (February 14, 2019) https://honestreporting.com/how-criticize-israel-without-being-antisemitic/

16 Kenrya Rankin, "Watch the UN Speech That Got Marc Lamont Hill Fired From CNN," (November 30, 2018) https://www.colorlines.com/articles/watch-un-speech-got-marc-lamont-hill-fired-cnn

17 Title VI is a section of the Civil Rights Act of 1964 ensuring protection from discrimination based on race or ethnicity. What Stern is objecting to (and we wholly agree) is the use of Title VI by those claiming that "Jewish" is a racial marker, Israel is the home for Jews, and therefore criticism of Israel (including BDS) is racist under Title VI, and therefore should be banned on college and university campuses. This is one of many methods employed by the pro-Israel lobby to shut down anti-Israel protests on college and university campuses.

18 Robert Mackey, "Trump Accuses Most American Jews of "Disloyalty" to Israel, Deploying Anti-Semitic Trope,"

The Intercept, (August 20, 2019) https://theintercept.com/2019/08/20/trump-jews-disloyalty-democratic-anti-semitism/

19 Noah Berlatsky, "Is Bernie Sanders anti-Semitic? Why new rightwing smears are the real anti-Semitism," NBC News – Think, (December 17, 2019) ohttps://www.nbcnews.com/think/opinion/bernie-sanders-jewish-liberal-probably-anti-semitic-according-right-ncna1103036

20 Tina Lowe, "Bernie Sanders has an anti-Semitism problem," *Washington Examiner* (December 13, 2019) https://www.washingtonexaminer.com/opinion/bernie-sanders-campaign-has-an-anti-semitism-problem

21 Ryan Autullo, "Judge rules against anti-Israel boycott law," *Austin American-Statesman*, (April 25, 2019) https://www.statesman.com/news/20190425/federal-judge-rules-against-texas-in-ban-on-boycotting-israel

22 For a deeper understanding of the effect anti-BDS legislation in the United states, see the film *Boycott* (2021) Directed by Julia Bacha, produced by Just Vision.

23 Ed Pilkington, "Revealed: Right-wing push to suppress criticism of Israel on US campuses." *The Guardian*, (October 17, 2019) https://www.theguardian.com/us-news/2019/oct/16/conservative-activists-want-to-outlaw-antisemitism-in-public-education-why-is-that-a-bad-thing

24 Matthew Rozsa, "Is Donald Trump a supporter of Israel? Sure — he's also an anti-Semite," Salon, (December 14, 2019) https://www.salon.com/2019/12/14/is-donald-trump-a-supporter-of-israel-sure-hes-also-an-anti-semite/

25 Jews made up about 35 percent of the population of Palestine but were given 58 percent of the land in the UN partition plan. Jews often counter this argument, noting that much of the land was in the Negev desert. While it is difficult to sort through the various versions of reality here, the population and land figures are generally agreed upon, but what they mean and if they were fair are widely disputed.

26 Israel also participated in a war in 1956 alongside Britain and France against Egypt, known as the Suez War or the Suez Crisis, also known

as the Second Arab-Israeli War. It led to a shift in the military power structure in the Middle East, diminishing Britain's imperial power and giving Egyptian leader Gamal Abdel Nassar a great deal more power and influence in the region.

27 Webinar, "Asking the Hard Questions: Preparing for the Joint Memorial Day Ceremony," The Parents Circle-Families Forum, March 2021, https://www.youtube.com/watch?v=p_xj25VTllo&t=13s

28 Wilkinson, Jeffrey, J "Israel/Palestine Experience and Engagement: A Multidirectional Study of Collective Memory Through an Analysis of Trauma, Identity and Victim Beliefs," University of Toronto, 2017

29 *The Holocaust and the Nakba: A New Grammar of Trauma and History*, editors B. Bashir and A. Goldberg, Columbia University Press, 2018.

30 Film: *Apolis* (2017), TELOS group https://vimeo.com/219903761

31 Noah Summers, "The Telos Group's Palestinian Propaganda Posing as Promotion of Peacemaking," *The Algemeiner* (July 21, 2017), https://www.algemeiner.com/2017/07/21/american-peacemaking-group-shills-palestinian-propaganda/

32 From: Englander, L. and Davids, S. *The Fragile Dialogue: New Voices of Liberal Zionism*. CCAR Press, 2017.

33 Webinar, "Where Things Stand at the Start of the Biden Presidency," Sponsored by the Foundation for Middle East Peace (FMEP), January 29, 2021.

34 The story of Passover, from the book of Exodus in the Old Testament. In the story, ten plagues are visited on the Egyptians in order to force Pharaoh to let the Jews go free. The final plague is the killing of the first-born Egyptian males, including Pharaoh's son. This is why the first-born Jewish sons still fast today at the beginning of Passover, up until the first seder meal.

35 Stephen Harper, "Why Don't You Support Israel?," PragerU. https://www.youtube.com/watch?v=tXy4NXbuE-k&t=15s

36 Peter Beinart, "I No Longer Believe in a Jewish State," *The New York Times*, (July 8, 2020)

37 "Statistics on Administrative Detention," B'Tselem , (November 24, 2021), https://www.btselem.org/administrative_detention/statistics

38 "6,000 Palestinian Children Jailed in Israel Since 2015: NGO," (April 15, 2019) https://www.aljazeera.com/news/2019/04/6000-palestinian-children-jailed-israel-2015-ngo-190405162640479.html

39 Judd Yadid, "Word of the Day: Tov Lamut Be'ad Artzeinu," *Haaretz*, (July 3, 2013) https://www.haaretz.com/. premium-word-of-the-day-tov-lamut-be-ad-artzeinu-1.5290158.

40 Mohammed Daraghmeh and Josef Federman, "Palestinian protest icon goes from jail cell to VIP suite," *The Times of Israel* (October 21, 2018) https://www.timesofisrael.com/palestinian-protest-icon-goes-from-jail-cell-to-vip-suite/

41 "Ahed Tamini: One story, multiple narratives," Al Jazeera English, (March 4, 2018) https://www.youtube.com/watch?v=HWEGUHpafsY

42 https://www.youtube.com/watch?v=HWEGUHpafsY

43 https://apnews.com/article/europe-middle-east-ap-top-news-israel-celebrity-33442ee79b064e73a2e440f97257cd8e

44 Zack Beauchamp, "Why the US has the most pro-Israel foreign policy in the world," Vox, (July 14, 2014) https://www.vox.com/2014/7/24/5929705/us-israel-friends

45 The term "Palestine" appears in written records as early as the fifth century BCE in the *Histories* of Herodotus. https://www.ancient.eu/palestine/

46 "Palestinian Liberation Organization", Palestine Remix (Al Jazeera), (Retrieved, July 3, 2021) https://interactive.aljazeera.com/aje/palestineremix/plo.html

47 Caroline B. Glick, "Column One: Mowing the lawn in Gaza," *The Jerusalem Post*, (October 18, 2018) https://www.jpost.com/opinion/column-one-mowing-the-lawn-in-gaza-569775

48 Ariel Ben Solomon, "Mowing the grass in Gaza," *Jewish National Syndicate*, (October 19, 2018) https://www.jns.org/opinion/mowing-the-grass-in-gaza/

49 Reem Kassis, "Here's why Palestinians object to the term 'Israeli food': It erases us from history," *The Washington Post*, (February 18, 2020) https://www.washingtonpost.com/lifestyle/food/heres-why-palestinians-object-to-the-term-israeli-food-it-erases-us-from-history/2020/02/14/96974a74-4d25-11ea-bf44-f5043eb3918a_story.html

50 Ronit Vered, "With 'Falastin,' Chef Sami Tamimi Redefines Palestinian Cuisine," *Haaretz*, (July 9, 2020) https://www.haaretz.com/israel-news/.premium.MAGAZINE-with-falastin-chef-sami-tamimi-redefines-palestinian-cuisine-1.8982831

51 Megan Jelinger, "Stitching tradition and modernity," Electronic Intifada, (May 28, 2018) https://electronicintifada.net/content/stitching-tradition-and-modernity/24461

52 Jessica Steinberg "When the keffiyeh turned couture," The Times of Israel, (October 22, 2015) https://www.timesofisrael.com/when-the-keffiyeh-turned-couture/

53 Eugénie Trochu, "Rencontre avec Dorit Baror, créatrice de Dodo Bar Or," Vogue France (April 23, 2015) http://www.vogue.fr/mode/portrait/diaporama/rencontre-avec-dorit-baror-cratrice-de-dodo-bar-or/20191

54 "Outrage as Israeli designer 'eroticises' Palestinian keffiyeh," The Observers, (April 2, 2016) https://observers.france24.com/en/20160204-israeli-designer-eroticization-palestinian-keffiyeh

55 Immigration to the United States 1933–41, United States Holocaust Memorial Museum, (Retrieved May 5, 2021) https://encyclopedia.ushmm.org/content/en/article/immigration-to-the-united-states-1933-41.

56 Lyndsay Van Dyck, "Canadian Immigration Acts and Legislation," Canadian Museum of Immigration, Pier 21, (Retrieved April 28, 2021) https://pier21.ca/research/immigration-history/canadian-immigration-acts-and-legislation#:~:text=The%20Chinese%20Immigration%20Act%20of,person%20seeking%20entry%20into%20Canada.&text=In%201900%2C%20the%20duty%20increased,increase%20to%20%24500%20in%201903.

57 "The Evian Conference," Facing History and Ourselves, (Retrieved May 5, 2021) https://www.facinghistory.org/resource-library/evian-conference.

58 See *Israel/Palestine Experience and Engagement: A multidirectional study of collective memory through and analysis of identity, trauma and victim beliefs,* Wilkinson, J., 2016. (Available at https://4acb41a0-b0e1-4766-9f12-c6b750fc7a9f.filesusr.com/ugd/10a264_064774513623465799b922aec81a7d56.pdf)

59 "Statement by the Prime Minister on Israel Independence Day," Prime Minister's Office, (April 15, 2021) https://pm.gc.ca/en/news/statements/2021/04/15/statement-prime-minister-israel-independence-day

60 "US lawmakers urge maintaining Israeli aid without preconditions," Al Jazeera, (April 21, 2021) https://www.aljazeera.com/news/2021/4/23/over-300-us-lawmakers-urge-continued-israel-aid-without-condition

61 For two vivid examples of the conflation of anti-Zionism and antisemitism (or anti-Semitism), - "The New Antisemitism." see:

   Irwin Cotler, "Defining the new anti-Semitism", The National Post (November 9, 2010) https://nationalpost.com/full-comment/irwin-cotler-defining-the-new-anti-semitism

   Brett Stephens, "Yes, anti-Zionism is anti-Semitism," The National Post (November 28, 2019) https://nationalpost.com/opinion/bret-stephens-yes-anti-zionism-is-anti-semitism

62 https://peterbeinart.substack.com/p/why-dov-hikind-thinks-im-pathetic Retrieved June 12, 2021

63 Peter Beinart, "Why Dov Hikind Thinks I'm "Pathetic" and "Sick," The Beinart Notebook (April 12, 2021) https://peterbeinart.substack.com/p/why-dov-hikind-thinks-im-pathetic

64 Karmi, "Land day: Israel's program of Palestinian land theft goes on undisturbed," Middle East Eye, (March 30, 2021) http://clients.intertech.ps/dci/en/Article/18046/March-30,-2021---Middle-East-Eye-Land-day-Israel's-programme-of-Palestinian-land-theft-goes-on-undisturbed-(By-Ghada-Karmi)

65 Wordsense Dictionary, (Retrieved July 23, 202)
    https://www.wordsense.eu/hasbara/

66 Yonatan Mendel, "Israel's 'Public' Diplomacy," London Review of Books,
    Vol. 32 No. 5, (March 11, 2010), https://www.lrb.co.uk/the-paper/v32/
    n05/yonatan-mendel/hasbara

67 Erum Salam, "Black Lives Matter protesters make Palestinian struggle
    their own," The Guardian, (June 16, 2020)
    https://www.theguardian.com/world/2021/jun/16/black-lives-matter-
    palestinian-struggle-us-left.

68 Idle No More, (Retrieved June 28, 2021) https://idlenomore.ca/
    idle-no-more-stands-in-solidarity-with-palestinian-people/

69 Fadel Allassan, "Over 500 ex-staffers urge Biden to 'hold Israel
    accountable for its actions'," Axios, (May 24, 2021) https://www.
    axios.com/israel-biden-palestinians-c3c0f372-156e-4be4-9390-
    05f976208a96.html.

70 "Open Letter, 680 leaders call on Joe Biden to take action to end
    Israeli Domination" Medecins du Monde, (June 3, 2021) https://
    www.medecinsdumonde.org/en/actualites/tribunes/2021/06/03/
    open-letter-joe-biden-israel-palestine-coalition

71 Laura Kelly, "Progressive groups call for Biden to denounce evictions
    of Palestinians as 'war crimes'," The Hill (June 3, 2021) https://thehill.
    com/policy/international/553472-more-than-100-progressive-groups-
    call-for-biden-to-denounce-evictions-of?rl=1

72 Sanjana Karanth, "138 House Democrats Demand Biden Call For
    A Cease-Fire In Israel," Huffpost, (May 19, 2021) https://www.
    huffpost.com/entry/house-democrats-demand-biden-call-ceasefire-
    israel_n_60a5bc6fe4b0a24c4f779b70

73 Oliver Holmes and Peter Beaumont, "Israeli police storm al-Aqsa
    mosque ahead of Jerusalem Day march," The Guardian (May 10, 2021)
    https://www.theguardian.com/world/2021/may/10/dozens-injured-in-
    clashes-over-israeli-settlements-ahead-of-jerusalem-day-march

74 Josef Federman and Fares Akram, "Beefed-up Israeli police clash with Palestinians in Jerusalem," Los Angeles Times, (May 7, 2021) https://www.latimes.com/world-nation/story/2021-05-07/palestinians-israel-police-clash-at-al-aqsa-mosque-53-hurt.

75 Merriam-Webster Dictionary, (Retrieved July 19, 2021) https://www.merriam-webster.com/dictionary/justice. Retrieved July 19, 2021

76 Two specific studies of young Jews in North America, one from 2013 from the Pew Research Center, https://www.pewforum.org/2013/10/01/jewish-american-beliefs-attitudes-culture-survey/, (retrieved February, 2021), and one Canadian study from the Jewish Federations of Canada from 2018 https://cdn.fedweb.org/fed-10/2/2017%252006%252004%2520Analysis%2520of%2520Under%252040%2520Survey.pdf, (retrieved February, 2021), show a general detachment from Israel compared with their parents and grandparents. However, these studies display a considerable variance in the attitudes of younger Jews. The Canadian study in particular seems to be geared to show that young Jews still feel a close bond to Israel. Our many conversations with younger Jews suggested that they are much more likely to want to move on from the traumas of the past and are upset with the Occupation and general treatment of Palestinians.

77 Israel and Antisemitism, "The Nexus Document: Understanding Antisemitism At Its Nexus With Israel And Zionism" (Retrieved November 5, 2021) https://israelandantisemitism.com/the-nexus-document/

78 JDA, "The Jerusalem Declaration on Antisemitism," (Retrieved November 5, 2021) https://jerusalemdeclaration.org/

BIBLIOGRAPHY AND SUGGESTED FURTHER READING

Bashir, B. and Goldberg, A. (Eds.) (2018) *The Holocaust and the Nakba: A New Grammar of Trauma and History*, Columbia University Press.

Bialystock, F. (2010). *Delayed Impact: The Holocaust and the Canadian Jewish Community*. Montreal: McGill-Queen's University Press.

Dawidowicz, L.S. (1975). *The War Against the Jews, 1935–1945*. New York: Holt, Rinehart and Winston.

Maalouf, A. (2011). *In the Name of Identity: Violence and the Need to Belong*. New York: Arcade.

Carroll, J. (2001). *Constantine's Sword: The Church and the Jews: A History*. New York: Houghton Mifflin

Caplan, N. (2009). *The Israeli-Palestinian Conflict: Contested Histories (Contesting the Past)*, Chichester: Wiley-Blackwell.

Caplan, N. (2019). *The Israeli–Palestinian Conflict: Contested Histories, 2nd Edition*. Hoboken Wiley-Blackwell.

Dan, M. *The Two-Sate Dilemma: A Game Theory Perspective on the Israeli-Palestinian Conflict*. Toronto: Barlow Book Publishing.

Haidt, J. and Lukianoff, G. (2018). *The Coddling of the American Mind: How Good Intentions and Bad Ideas Are Setting Up a Generation for Failure*. New York: Penguin Press.

Halkin, H. (2014). *Jabotinsky: A Life*. New Haven: Yale University Press.

McGowan, D. and Ellis, M. (Eds.) (1998) *Remembering Deir Yassin: The Future of Israel and Palestine*, Olive Branch Press.

Pawel, E. (1989). *The Labyrinth of Exile: A Life of Theodor Herzl*. New York: Farrar, Straus & Giroux.

Said, E. (1978) *Orientalism*. New York: Random House Inc.

Scieszka, J. (1996). *The True Story of the Three Little Pigs*. New York: Penguin Books.

Said, E. (1978) *Orientalism*. New York: Random House Inc.

Stern, K. (2020). *The Conflict Over the Conflict: The Israel/Palestine Campus Debate*. Toronto: New Jewish Press.

Troper, H and Abella, I. (1982). *None Is Too Many: Canada and the Jews of Europe, 1933–1948*. Toronto: Key Porter Books.

APPENDIX:
SUGGESTED QUESTIONS FOR DISCUSSION GROUPS OR BOOK CLUBS

PART I – BUILDING THE WALL: SHAPING THE NARRATIVE

Chapter 1 - How We Come to "Know"
Chapter 2 - Memory Is More Than What Happened
Chapter 3 - The Mortar in the Wall: Identity, Trauma, and Victimhood

1. How do you see confirmation bias and belief perseverance in your circle of family, friends, and colleagues?
2. Within the Israel-Palestine context, what particular information might feel threatening to you and why?
3. What have you learned about the difference between facts and personal truths? What factors play into creating one's personal truths?
4. Understanding how identity, trauma, and victimhood operate in forming resistance to the Other, talk about the resulting tribalism in the Israel-Palestine context.

PART II — THE BRICKS IN THE WALL: COMPETING NARRATIVES

Chapter 4 - Antisemitism

1. Reflect on how a Jew and a Palestinian react differently to the word "antisemitism."
2. How has the charge of antisemitism impacted Palestinians' ability to resist their oppression?
3. How has the continued presence of antisemitism affected Jewish sentiment towards Israel?

Chapter 5 - Zionism and the Nakba

1. Zionism has an entirely different connotation for Jews than it does for Palestinians. Discuss these two competing views and whether or not they are reconcilable.
2. Progressive Zionists, believing that Palestinians deserve self-determination in the same manner as Jews do, see the root of the problem as the occupation and settlement expansion (post-1967), while Palestinians see the root of their oppression as the Nakba (1948). Why do you think this difference in perspective persists?
3. Discuss the trauma, for Jews and for Palestinians, that has resulted from two distinct events: the Holocaust and the Nakba.

Chapter 6 - Palestinian Resistance

1. Over there, Palestinians call it resistance; Israelis call it terrorism—discuss.
2. Over here, the struggle about the struggle is as ferocious as it is over there, while mostly nonviolent. Discuss how the framework of "mainstream muscularity" and "marginalized resistance" play out in the struggle over here.

PART III – HARDENING THE WALL: WEAPONIZING THE NARRATIVE

Chapter 7 - Jewish Exceptionalism and Palestinian Otherness
Chapter 8 - Weaponizing Tribalism

1. How did empathy towards Jews in the West, emanating from guilt over a history of antisemitism and the tragedy of the Holocaust, influence how Western society perceives the Israel-Palestine struggle?
2. How has the stereotypical image of the brown Arab/ Muslim as fanatic and terroristic impacted western society's perception of the Israel-Palestine struggle?
3. How have the action of "BADD" actors impacted our discourse around the Israel-Palestine struggle in the West?
4. How has the language that lobby groups use to frame antisemitism and Palestinian resistance influenced you personally?

PART IV – DISMANTLING THE WALL: THE MAKING OF A NEW NARRATIVE

Chapter 9 - Towards Values-Forward Thinking
Chapter 10 - Working in Spaces Where the Narratives Collide

1. Describe the challenges you may encounter in uncoupling from trauma and propaganda and shifting towards values-forward thinking.
2. Describe how your thinking may have shifted as a result of reading this book?
3. Describe one action that you personally will take in response to the transformative questions presented in Chapter 10.

ABOUT THE AUTHORS

Jeffrey J. Wilkinson, PhD, is an American Jew who lives in Canada. He holds a doctorate in Education from the University of Toronto and works actively in the Jewish community and beyond on issues relating to trauma and the Israel/Palestine struggle. Jeff's partnership with Raja, borne out of deep listening and learning together, has become central to his work.

Raja G. Khouri is CEO of Khouri Conversations, a human rights and inclusion consultant, the founding president of the Canadian Arab Institute, board member at Project Rozana (Canada), and a former 10-year commissioner with the Ontario Human Rights Commission. He is a Canada Committee member of Human Rights Watch, and co-founder of the Canadian Arab/Jewish Leadership Dialogue Group.